BLURᴸ

Embark on a profound odyssey of self-discovery and spiritual enlightenment with 'Chakra Evolution'—a captivating voyage into the depths of the mystical realms within. Delve into the essence of what it truly means to embody the crystalline nature of existence as you chart the evolution of your chakra centres. Explore the intricate pathways of your energetic system, unraveling the profound wisdom encoded within each energy vortex.

Within these pages, you'll uncover transformative tools and practices designed to heal trauma wounds and dismantle restrictive patterns that obstruct the free flow of energy. Discover how to protect your energy body and recognise the symptoms of ascension as you navigate the ebbs and flows of your spiritual journey, finding balance and empowerment in every step.

With breathtaking illustrations illuminating the path to enlightenment, 'Chakra Evolution' invites you to ignite your inner light and awaken to new dimensions of conscious living. Through personal anecdotes and timeless wisdom, this book offers a transformative journey of self-realisation and spiritual growth. Are you ready to embark on this luminous adventure and illuminate the cosmos within?

CHAKRA EVOLUTION

THE GENESIS OF CONSCIOUS ASCENSION

N.J. POWELL

Within the depths of cosmic consciousness lies the radiant essence of our being, awaiting illumination through the awakening of the chakras.

— UNKNOWN

CONTENTS

INTRODUCTION

In the vast landscape of spiritual exploration, the concept of 'Becoming Crystalline' emerges as a guiding beacon, illuminating the path of personal and collective evolution. Rooted in metaphorical interpretations of spiritual growth and enlightenment, this concept resonates deeply within New Age circles, offering seekers of truth and wisdom a beacon of hope and transformation.

Have you ever pondered the depths of your inner being, wondering what lies beyond the surface of your consciousness?

Imagine tapping into an infinite wellspring of energy and knowledge within yourself, a boundless reservoir waiting to be awakened. What if I told you that this energy holds the key to unlocking your true potential and illuminating the path to profound self-discovery? As you ponder the depths of your inner being, consider the concept of 'becoming crystalline'—a guiding beacon in the vast landscape of spiritual exploration.

Delve into the essence of what it truly means to embody the crystalline nature of existence as you chart the evolution of your chakra centres. Explore the intricate pathways of your energetic system, unraveling the profound wisdom encoded within each energy vortex. Uncover transformative tools and practices designed to heal trauma wounds and dismantle restrictive patterns that obstruct the free flow of energy.

Discover how to protect your energy body and recognise the symptoms of ascension as you navigate the ebbs and flows of your spiritual journey, finding balance and empowerment in every step.

With breathtaking illustrations enhancing the path to enlightenment, 'Chakra Evolution' invites you to ignite your inner light and awaken to new dimensions of conscious living. Through personal anecdotes and timeless wisdom, this book offers a transformative journey of self-realisation and spiritual growth.

Visualise yourself on the shore of an expansive, shimmering sea, its depths holding the promise of boundless exploration. Embarking on the journey toward becoming crystalline is akin to plunging into those depths, delving into the innermost layers of our being to reveal the radiant clarity that resides within.

As we set forth on the adventure of 'Chakra Evolution', I invite you to join on this profound exploration of self-discovery and spiritual awakening. Through the lens of our chakra system, we will navigate the intricate pathways of energy, unlocking the secrets of our spiritual evolution and deepening our understanding of the interconnectedness of all things.

Within these pages, you'll find practical insights into activating the chakras, enhancing energy, and safeguarding your energy system, all while expanding consciousness along the way.

By embracing the transformative power of 'Chakra Evolution', we can awaken to our true nature and embark on a journey of spiritual growth and self-realisation.

Are you ready to dive deep into the shimmering depths of your soul, to uncover the radiant clarity that lies within, and to illuminate both the inner and outer cosmos? If so, then let us embark together on this luminous odyssey.

THE ART OF MINDFUL MEDITATION

*W*elcome to 'Chakra Evolution,' a journey into the depths of the metaphysical body through the art of mindful meditation. In this book, we will embark on an exploration of the chakras and their evolution, those swirling energy centres within us that hold the key to our spiritual and emotional well-being.

MEDITATION IS OFTEN SEEN as a path to inner peace and relaxation, but it is also a powerful tool for delving into the mysteries of our metaphysical body. To truly understand and connect with our chakras, we must learn to cultivate both stillness of mind and the power of visualisation.

IN THE PAGES AHEAD, we will delve into the practice of mindful meditation, where we learn to quiet the chatter of our busy minds and tune into the subtle energies that flow within us. This process may require patience and dedication, as we learn to navigate the depths of our inner landscape. We will also explore a visualisation guide to help channel our consciousness into our energy system.

AT FIRST, our meditation practice may focus solely on achieving stillness of mind, learning to let go of the distractions and worries that so often cloud our thoughts. But as we become more adept at entering into a state of mindfulness, we can begin to introduce visualisation techniques that will guide us into the realm of the metaphysical body.

VISUALISATIONS ACT as a bridge between the conscious mind and the subtle energies of the chakras, allowing us to access deeper layers of awareness and insight. As we progress on our journey, these visualisations become more than just mental images – they become gateways to profound states of connection and transformation.

AS YOU EMBARK on this journey through 'Chakra Evolution,' remember that meditation is a practice – one that requires patience, persistence, and an open heart. Allow yourself to surrender to the process, knowing that with each moment of stillness and each visualisation, you are drawing closer to the radiant essence of your true self.

THE JOURNEY TO STILLNESS

Embark on a transformative journey toward inner peace and clarity as we explore the profound practice of meditation. In this chapter, we delve into practical techniques to quiet the mind, cultivate present-moment awareness, and unlock the boundless serenity within. Discover how meditation not only enhances mental and emotional well-being but also facilitates the exploration of the metaphysical body and the evolution of the chakras.

UNDERSTANDING the Mind

At the heart of our being lies a ceaseless stream of thoughts, weaving a web that obscures the path to deeper states of consciousness. Acknowledging this perpetual flux, we delve into techniques aimed at quieting the mind and ushering in the serenity of stillness. By quieting the mind, we create space for exploration of the metaphysical body and the evolution of the chakras.

THE PRACTICE of Letting Go

Central to the journey of stillness is the practice of letting go —an act of profound surrender to the flow of existence. By relinquishing attachment to thoughts, emotions, and perceptions as they arise, we create spaciousness within, paving the way for the emergence of inner tranquility.

CULTIVATING Present-Moment Awareness

Anchor yourself in the present moment as a potent antidote to the relentless stream of mental noise. Through focused attention on the breath or bodily sensations, transcend the cacophony of the mind, stepping into the silent sanctum of pure awareness. This heightened awareness facilitates the exploration of the metaphysical body and the subtle nuances of the chakras.

ADDITIONAL VARIATIONS OF MEDITATION TECHNIQUES

While the meditation practices covered in this chapter offer valuable tools for cultivating stillness and exploring the metaphysical body, it's important to recognise that there are many paths to inner peace and self-discovery. In addition to traditional methods, consider exploring additional variations of meditation techniques that cater to different preferences and skill levels, including creative endeavours.

BREATH AWARENESS MEDITATION

- Let the rhythmic dance of the breath guide you in the journey to stillness. With mindful awareness, observe each inhalation and exhalation, allowing the mind to gently settle into a state of profound calm. As you deepen your breath awareness, you also deepen your connection to the metaphysical body and the energy flow within the chakras.

Mantra Meditation

- Seek solace from the chaotic waves of thoughts by engaging in the sacred practice of repeating a chosen mantra. Allow these sacred words to resonate within you, acting as a guiding light that leads you to the serene depths of consciousness. Mantra meditation serves not only as a focal point but also as a potent method for delving into the metaphysical realm and aligning the chakras harmoniously.

Sound Meditation

- Engage your auditory senses in the practice of meditation by incorporating sound-based techniques. This could involve listening to calming music, nature sounds, or chanting mantras. Allow the vibrations of sound to wash over you, guiding your mind into a state of deep relaxation and heightened awareness.

Movement Meditation

- For those who find it challenging to sit still during meditation, movement-based practices offer an alternative approach. Tai chi, qigong, walking meditation, or yoga can all be forms of movement meditation. Focus on the rhythm of your movements, syncing them with your breath, and cultivating mindfulness as you flow through each motion.

Creative Meditation

- Tap into your creative spirit by integrating artistic expression into your meditation practice. This could involve activities such as painting, drawing, writing, or even gardening. Allow yourself to immerse fully in the creative process, letting go of judgment and self-criticism as you explore your inner world through artistry.

Guided Imagery

- Embark on a journey of the imagination with guided imagery meditation. Listen to recordings or read scripts that lead you through vivid visualisations of peaceful landscapes, healing encounters, or journeys to your inner sanctuary. Allow your mind to wander freely as you engage your senses in this immersive mental exploration.

Loving-Kindness Meditation

- Cultivate compassion and empathy through loving-kindness meditation, also known as Metta meditation. Focus on generating feelings of love, kindness, and goodwill toward yourself, loved ones, acquaintances, and even difficult individuals. Repeat phrases or affirmations that evoke feelings of warmth and acceptance, fostering a sense of interconnectedness with all beings.

Progressive Muscle Relaxation

- Release tension and promote relaxation throughout your entire body with progressive muscle relaxation. Begin by tensing and then slowly releasing each muscle group, starting from your toes and working your way up to your head. Notice the sensations of warmth and heaviness as you surrender to a state of deep relaxation.

Mindful Eating

- Transform an everyday activity into a mindfulness practice with mindful eating meditation. Slow down and savour each bite of food, paying close attention to the colours, textures, flavours, and sensations experienced with each mouthful. Cultivate gratitude for the nourishment provided by your meal and the interconnectedness of all beings involved in its creation.

Nature Meditation

- Connect with the natural world through nature meditation. Find a quiet outdoor spot where you can sit or walk mindfully amidst the beauty of the earth. Tune in to the sights, sounds, smells, and sensations of the natural environment, allowing it to ground you and evoke a sense of peace and harmony.

Breath work Variations

- Explore different breath work techniques to deepen your meditation practice. Alternatives to traditional breath awareness meditation include square breathing, alternate nostril breathing, or the 4-7-8 breathing technique. Experiment with various rhythms and patterns of breathing to discover what resonates most with your body and mind.

BENEFITS OF MEDITATION

Beyond the profound experiences of stillness and inner exploration, meditation offers a plethora of benefits for overall well-being. Regular meditation practice has been scientifically proven to reduce stress, alleviate symptoms of anxiety and depression, improve focus and concentration, enhance emotional resilience, and promote feelings of inner peace and contentment. Moreover, meditation has been shown to positively impact physical health by lowering blood pressure, boosting the immune system, and promoting better sleep. By integrating meditation into your daily routine, you cultivate a greater sense of balance, harmony, and vitality in all aspects of your life.

· · ·

CULTIVATING stillness in meditation is an ever-unfolding odyssey —a sacred pilgrimage of the soul. Through the practice of letting go, the cultivation of present-moment awareness, and the exploration of diverse meditation techniques, transcend the distractions of the mind and discover the boundless serenity that resides within. Embrace meditation as a gateway to the exploration of the metaphysical body and the evolution of the chakras, unlocking the transformative power of self-discovery and spiritual growth.

BY EMBRACING a diverse range of meditation techniques, individuals can find the practices that resonate most deeply with their unique preferences, personalities, and intentions. Whether through sound, movement, creativity, or mindfulness, each variation offers a pathway to inner peace, self-discovery, and spiritual growth.

* * *

LUCID DREAMING VISUALISATION MEDITATION FOR ACCESSING THE ENERGY BODY AND CHAKRAS

Lucid dreaming offers a gateway to exploring not only the dream world but also the realms of our energy body and chakras. This visualisation meditation is designed to guide you into a lucid dream state where you can connect with your energy centres and experience profound healing and alignment. By practicing this meditation regularly, you can enhance your awareness of the subtle energies within and awaken the power of your chakras.

VISUALISATION MEDITATION

Deepen your meditation experience by incorporating visualisation techniques that invite exploration beyond the physical realm.

PREPARATION

- Find a quiet and comfortable space where you can sit or lie down without distractions. Close your eyes and take a few deep breaths to centre yourself.

Visualisation Journey

- Close your eyes, directing your gaze to the third eye point—the seat of intuition and inner vision—and create a canvas for the imagination to unfold. Visualisations can lead to profound insights into the metaphysical body and the energetic dynamics of the chakras.

GROUNDING at the Root Chakra

- Visualise yourself standing in a tranquil garden surrounded by lush greenery and vibrant flowers. Feel the warmth of the sun on your skin and the soft earth beneath your feet as you ground yourself in this sacred space.

- Focus your attention on the base of your spine, where the root chakra is located. Visualise a glowing red energy vortex spinning gently at the base of your spine, anchoring you to the earth and providing a sense of stability and security.

• With each inhale, imagine drawing in fresh, revitalising energy from the earth, allowing it to flow up through your feet and into your root chakra. Feel this energy grounding and nourishing you, strengthening your connection to the physical world.

ACTIVATION of the Sacral Chakra

• Shift your awareness to the area just below your navel, where the sacral chakra resides. Envision a warm, orange light glowing brightly in this area, radiating creativity, passion, and pleasure.

• As you breathe deeply, visualise the energy of the sacral chakra expanding and flowing freely throughout your body, igniting your creative spark and awakening your sensual nature.

EMPOWERMENT at the Solar Plexus Chakra

• Move upward, focusing your attention on the solar plexus, located in the upper abdomen. Picture a vibrant yellow sun glowing at this centre, filling you with confidence, personal power, and inner strength.

- With each breath, allow the energy of the solar plexus chakra to grow brighter and more luminous, empowering you to assert your will and pursue your dreams with courage and determination.

EXPANSION of the Heart Chakra

- Continue to ascend to the heart centre, located in the centre of your chest. Visualise a beautiful emerald green light emanating from this chakra, enveloping you in a warm embrace of love, compassion, and forgiveness.

- Feel your heart opening and expanding with each breath, radiating love and light outward to all beings and receiving the love of the universe in return. Allow this energy to heal past wounds and awaken a profound sense of connection and unity with all of creation.

EXPRESSION through the Throat Chakra

- Direct your awareness to the throat chakra, situated at the base of your throat. Imagine a bright blue light shining here, empowering you to speak your truth with clarity, authenticity, and integrity.

- With each breath, feel the energy of the throat chakra expanding, clearing any blockages and allowing your authentic voice to be heard. Express yourself freely and confidently, knowing that your words have the power to create positive change in the world.

Awakening of the Third Eye Chakra

- Bring your focus to the third eye chakra, located between your eyebrows. Visualise a deep indigo light radiating from this centre, awakening your intuition, insight, and inner wisdom.

- As you breathe deeply, feel the energy of the third eye chakra opening and expanding, illuminating your path and guiding you toward greater understanding and enlightenment. Trust in your inner vision and allow it to lead you toward your highest purpose.

Connection with the Crown Chakra

- Finally, turn your attention to the crown chakra, situated at the top of your head. Envision a brilliant violet light shining here, connecting you to the divine source of all creation.

- With each breath, feel the energy of the crown chakra expanding upward, opening your consciousness to the infinite wisdom and boundless love of the universe. Surrender to the flow of divine energy and allow it to guide you toward spiritual awakening and enlightenment.

. . .

As you continue to practice this lucid dreaming visualisation meditation, you deepen your connection to your energy body and chakras, awakening their power and potential for healing and transformation. Trust in the wisdom of your inner self and allow yourself to explore the vast realms of consciousness within. With each journey into the dream world, you awaken to new levels of awareness and understanding, unlocking the secrets of your soul and embracing the fullness of your being.

JOURNALLING

As you embark on your meditation journey, consider keeping a meditation journal to track your progress, insights, and experiences. Journaling can serve as a valuable tool for self-reflection and growth, allowing you to capture fleeting moments of clarity and inspiration. Take time to write down your thoughts, observations, and reflections after each meditation session, noting any shifts in your awareness or experiences within the metaphysical body.

Remember, journalling does not have to be restricted to the written word. As an artist, I found the process of recreating what I saw during meditation to be valuable in my journey of understanding. Whether through words, drawings, paintings, or any other form of expression, documenting your journey allows you to create a tangible record of your growth and evolution, serving as a source of inspiration and guidance along the way.

Dream Interpretation and Cultural Symbols

Dream interpretation and understanding cultural symbols

can be valuable tools to enhance your meditation practice. Dreams often reflect the workings of the subconscious mind and the energies that influence our waking reality. Keeping a dream journal and reflecting on the symbols, themes, and emotions present in your dreams can uncover hidden truths about yourself and your spiritual journey.

Moreover, exploring cultural symbols from mythology, folklore, and spiritual traditions can provide deeper insights into the meaning behind your meditation experiences and the symbolism of the chakras. Take time to research and contemplate the cultural significance of symbols that resonate with you, allowing them to enrich your meditation practice and deepen your connection to the metaphysical body and the evolution of the chakras.

MEDITATION SERVES as a powerful gateway to the exploration of the metaphysical body and the evolution of the chakras. By delving into the depths of our consciousness through meditation, we unlock the transformative power of self-discovery and spiritual growth.

CULTURAL INSIGHTS INTO THE CHAKRA SYSTEM

*I*n our exploration of chakra evolution and the pursuit of crystalline consciousness, it's imperative to lay a robust foundation rooted in the rich tapestry of traditional wisdom. These traditions offer profound insights into the interconnectedness of the subtle body and the pivotal role of chakras in fostering holistic well-being.

BEFORE DELVING into the intricacies of chakra evolution, it's essential to recognise the cultural diversity and historical significance that underpin our understanding of these energy centres. Across Hinduism and various Eastern philosophies, chakras serve as the cornerstone of the subtle body, intricately interconnected and aligned along the central axis from the base of the spine to the crown of the head.

EACH CHAKRA HOLDS SPECIFIC QUALITIES, functions, and aspects of consciousness, playing a crucial role in physical, mental, emotional, and spiritual well-being.

OVERVIEW OF CHAKRAS IN HINDU AND EASTERN TRADITIONS

Let's embark on a concise overview of the seven main chakras, as commonly described in Hinduism and other Eastern traditions:

- **Root Chakra (Muladhara):** Associated with grounding and security, located at the base of the spine.

- **Sacral Chakra (Swadhisthana):** Linked to creativity and emotional balance, situated in the lower abdomen.

- **Solar Plexus Chakra (Manipura):** Related to personal power and confidence, positioned in the upper abdomen.

- **Heart Chakra (Anahata):** Associated with love and compassion, located in the centre of the chest.

- **Throat Chakra (Vishuddha):** Linked to communication and self-expression, positioned in the throat area.

- **Third Eye Chakra (Ajna):** Associated with intuition and inner wisdom, located between the eyebrows.

- **Crown Chakra (Sahasrara):** Related to spiritual connection and enlightenment, situated at the top of the head.

PRACTICES AND PHILOSOPHIES

In Eastern philosophies, the activation, alignment, and

balance of the chakras are considered fundamental for holistic well-being and spiritual growth. Practices such as yoga, meditation, breath work, and energy healing aim to awaken and harmonise the chakras, facilitating the flow of vital energy (Prana) throughout the body and promoting health, vitality, and spiritual evolution.

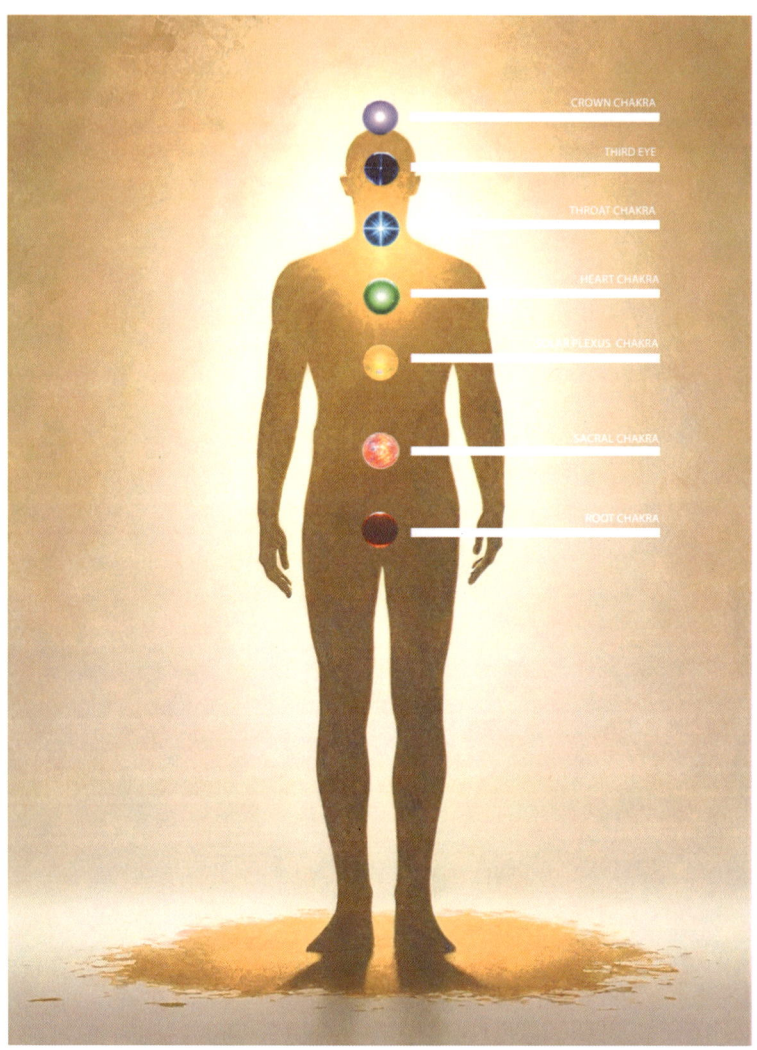

CROWN CHAKRA

THIRD EYE

THROAT CHAKRA

HEART CHAKRA

SOLAR PLEXUS CHAKRA

SACRAL CHAKRA

ROOT CHAKRA

Diagram representing chakra alignment on body - N.J. Powell

OTHER CULTURAL ENERGY BELIEFS

VARIOUS CULTURAL AND spiritual traditions offer teachings on energy centres akin to the concept of chakras. Let's explore a few examples

TAOIST TRADITION (CHINA)

Taoist alchemy and energy cultivation practices emphasise the concept of energy centres or "dantians." Through practices like Qigong and Tai Chi, practitioners aim to cultivate and refine their energy centres, leading to spiritual transformation and enlightenment.

KABBALAH (JEWISH MYSTICISM)

Kabbalistic teachings feature the "Tree of Life," depicting ten interconnected energy centres called Sephiroth. Activation and alignment of these centres are vital for spiritual growth and enlightenment.

NATIVE AMERICANS

Native American tribes hold diverse spiritual traditions, with varying beliefs about the energy body and subtle energy systems. Despite differences, many traditions share the concept of an interconnected energy web animating all life, linking beings to nature and the spiritual realm. They recognise a vital life force flowing through all living beings, known by different names like "spirit energy" or "life force." This energy, present in humans, animals, plants, and the Earth, is seen as the source of vitality and spiritual power. Various tribes have unique teachings on energy, such as "spirit paths" or "spirit lines" within the body, akin to energy channels found in other traditions. These paths facilitate the flow of spiritual energy, promoting health and harmony. Healing practices include ceremonies, rituals, and herbs aimed at cleansing and strengthening the energy body, like smudging and sweat lodge ceremonies. Despite variations, Native American traditions emphasise the interconnectedness of life forms and living in harmony with nature and spiritual realms, honouring the sacredness of all existence and recognising spirituality's role in healing and well-being.

THE ZULU CULTURE

The Zulu culture, like many indigenous societies, has rich spiritual traditions that include beliefs about energy systems within the body. They refer to this life force as "umoya," which is vital for vitality, consciousness, and spiritual power. Similar to other traditions, Zulu beliefs recognise subtle energy pathways facilitating umoya's flow, crucial for overall well-being. Zulu spiritual practices aim to align and cultivate umoya through rituals and ceremonies, promoting harmony and spiritual connection. Despite variations among communities, Zulu beliefs emphasise the interconnectedness of all beings and the importance of nurturing the spiritual dimension of existence for holistic well-being.

ANCIENT EGYPT

Ancient Egypt boasts a rich spiritual tradition centred around the concept of "ka" or "kꜣ," representing the life force akin to the soul or vital energy. This belief permeated their society, shaping their practices and rituals aimed at nurturing and safeguarding this essential aspect of being.

Egyptians entrusted the preservation of their ka to a range of ceremonial practices, often conducted by priests who held significant roles in spiritual matters. These rituals encompassed a wide array of activities, from offering prayers and incantations to performing elaborate ceremonies dedicated to the ka's well-being.

Amulets played a crucial role in Egyptian spiritual practices, believed to possess protective properties against negative energies and malevolent forces. These sacred objects were intricately crafted and imbued with potent symbolism, serving as tangible symbols of divine protection for the bearer's ka.

Through their reverence for the ka and meticulous attention to spiritual practices, the ancient Egyptians demonstrated a profound understanding of the interconnectedness between the physical and spiritual realms, striving to maintain harmony and balance within themselves and their cosmos.

ANCIENT GREECE

Ancient Greek philosophy, notably Plato and Aristotle, emphasised the soul's importance in understanding human existence, echoing aspects of the energy body concept. Within this context, the notion of "pneuma," meaning "breath" or "spirit," held significance in both philosophical and medical discourse. Philosophically, pneuma represented the vital life force permeating the universe, imbuing beings with consciousness and vitality. Heraclitus and Stoics saw it as a unifying principle governing the cosmos. Medically, figures like Hippocrates and Galen viewed pneuma as the body's vital force, circulating to maintain health. They described various types of pneuma associated with bodily functions. Pneuma flowed through channels or vessels in the body, akin to nadis or meridians in Eastern traditions. Imbalances or blockages in pneuma circulation could lead to illness, underscoring the need for harmony. In connection with energy centres or chakras, pneuma offers a parallel concept of vital energy sustaining life and connecting humans to the cosmos.

Exploring pneuma in Ancient Greek thought provides insights into ancient perceptions of the body's energetic nature and its impact on overall well-being, reflecting similar concepts found across diverse cultures and historical periods.

ANCIENT INDIA (VEDIC CIVILISATION)

The Vedic civilisation of ancient India, dating back thousands of years, had a sophisticated understanding of the subtle energy body. The Vedas, ancient Indian texts, describe the concept of "prana," or life force energy, which flows through channels known as nadis and converges at points called chakras. Practices like yoga, meditation, and Ayurveda were developed to balance and optimise the flow of prana for health and spiritual growth.

THESE ARE JUST A FEW EXAMPLES, but they demonstrate that the understanding of energy bodies and centres is not limited to modern or Eastern cultures. Many ancient civilisations had their own interpretations of these concepts, often rooted in spiritual and philosophical traditions that sought to understand the nature of existence and human consciousness.

BY STUDYING THESE DIVERSE PERSPECTIVES, we gain a deeper understanding of the evolution of energy centres within the body and their significance in various cultural contexts. The universal principles underlying spiritual growth and well-being are illuminated, inspiring us to continue our exploration of the chakra system across different traditions and cultures.

CRYSTALLINE ALCHEMY

*E*mbark on a journey through chakra evolution as we delve into the mysteries of crystalline consciousness—the foundational essence weaving through the intricate tapestry of our energetic anatomy and spiritual enlightenment. 'Crystalline consciousness' symbolises a state of heightened clarity, purity, and alignment with divine energy, representing the pinnacle of our spiritual evolution. In this transformative quest, we assimilate the qualities of crystals—clarity, amplification, and resonance—into the very fabric of our consciousness.

BEFORE DELVING DEEPER into the profound connection between chakra evolution and crystalline consciousness, let's establish a solid foundation by exploring the fundamentals of crystals in healing. This chapter serves as a grounding point, offering insights into the transformative power of crystals and their pivotal role in our journey towards enlightenment.

. . .

As we progress through the book, the significance of 'crystalline consciousness' as the root of our chakra development will become increasingly apparent. Each subsequent chapter peels back the layers of this profound concept, revealing its multifaceted nature and intrinsic connection to our spiritual evolution.

Navigating the pathways of our chakra system, we unlock the transformative potential encoded within each energy centre. Each chakra serves as a gateway to higher states of consciousness, imparting unique lessons and insights on the journey of self-discovery. By attuning and harmonising these energy centres, we align ourselves with the vibrational frequencies of the universe, paving the way for the emergence of crystalline consciousness.

Through chakra activation, alignment, and evolution, we purify and elevate our energetic vibration, shedding layers of conditioning and limitation to reveal our true essence. Deepening our understanding of the chakra system and cultivating practices to balance and harmonise these energy centres bring us closer to embodying the crystalline consciousness at our core.

Join me on this transformative odyssey, where the mysteries of crystalline consciousness await unraveling, and the radiant essence of our being beckons us toward profound self-discovery and ascension.

UNVEILING THE MYSTERIES OF CRYSTALS

Embarking on the journey to becoming crystalline requires us to delve deep into the essence of crystals—those captivating gems of the Earth that hold both physical and metaphysical significance. In this chapter, we'll unravel the secrets of crystals, exploring their intricate atomic structures, elemental compositions, and subtle energies that intertwine with our own.

THE ELEMENTAL SYMPHONY OF CRYSTALS

At the heart of every crystal lies a symphony of elements—fundamental building blocks that form the fabric of our Earth and our very being. Silicon, oxygen, carbon, calcium, and a myriad of others dance together in a harmonious lattice, echoing the rhythms of life itself. The elemental compositions of crystals uncover a profound connection between Earth's geological processes and the intricate biology of life. The primordial soup of creation.

HARNESSING THE ENERGY WITHIN

Beyond their physical allure, crystals possess a subtle energy that resonates with the electromagnetic field of the human body, offering pathways to balance, harmony, and well-being. While scientific exploration into the energetic properties of crystals is ongoing, centuries of anecdotal evidence within the realms of crystal healing affirm their transformative potential. From the gentle vibrations of amethyst to the soothing energies of rose quartz, crystals serve as allies on our journey of self-discovery and healing.

· · ·

IN MY PERSONAL JOURNEY, I've encountered the profound effects of crystals firsthand. One unforgettable moment stands out when I assisted my sound healer in moving her crystal bowl after a healing session. As I cradled the bowl in my arms, I was enveloped by an overwhelming sensation of love emanating from it. Overcome by the intensity of the vibrations, I had to pause and carefully set it down, fearing I might lose my grasp. That bowl, now etched in my memory with great love, became a conduit for a profound realisation of the immense potency of crystal energy. This experience illuminated the depth of their power and fuelled my passion to share their transformative benefits with others.

FOR THOSE NEW to working with crystals, I recommend starting with a few common varieties such as clear quartz, amethyst, and rose quartz. These versatile crystals are readily available and can be used for a variety of purposes, from promoting relaxation to enhancing intuition. When selecting crystals, trust your intuition and choose stones that resonate with you on a personal level.

ADVANCED CRYSTAL HEALING TECHNIQUES

As our understanding of crystals deepens, we uncover more advanced practices that harness their potent energies for profound healing and spiritual growth. These techniques delve into the intricate interplay between crystals and the human energy system, offering powerful tools for holistic well-being.

CRYSTAL HEALING LAYOUTS

Crystal healing layouts are sophisticated arrangements of crystals strategically placed on or around the body to target specific areas of imbalance or promote overall wellness. These layouts often incorporate sacred geometry and intuitive crystal selection to amplify healing intentions. For example, a crystal grid may be constructed around the body to create a harmonious energetic field, while individual crystals are positioned on corresponding chakras to balance and align their energies.

CHAKRA BALANCING with Crystals

Chakras, the energy centres within the body, play a vital role in our physical, emotional, and spiritual health. Advanced crystal healing techniques utilise crystals to cleanse, activate, and balance the chakras, restoring optimal energy flow and vitality. Practitioners may use specialised layouts or crystal wands to target specific chakras, employing crystals with corresponding colours and properties to facilitate healing and alignment.

WORKING with Crystal Wands or Grids

Crystal wands and grids offer versatile tools for deeper energetic work, allowing practitioners to focus and direct crystal energy with precision. Crystal wands, typically crafted from single or double-terminated crystals, are used to channel energy during healing sessions, clear energy blockages, and activate specific points on the body or within the energy field. Grids, on the other hand, involve arranging crystals in geometric patterns to amplify intentions and manifest desired outcomes. Advanced practitioners may combine crystal wands and grids to perform intricate energy work, accessing higher states of consciousness and facilitating profound spiritual transformation.

INTEGRATION AND EXPLORATION

As we delve into advanced crystal healing techniques, it's essential to approach these practices with reverence, mindfulness, and respect for the inherent wisdom of crystals. Integrating these techniques into our healing repertoire allows us to deepen our connection with the subtle energies of the universe and unlock new levels of healing and spiritual growth. Through continued exploration and practice, we harness the transformative power of crystals to illuminate our path toward wholeness and alignment with the divine.

WHETHER DRAWING from ancient traditions or crafting personalised ceremonies, the intention behind crystal rituals is to honour the sacredness of crystals and invite their healing energies into one's life with reverence and respect.

THE SYMPHONY OF VIBRATIONAL FREQUENCIES

In the realm of quantum mechanics and spectroscopy, the vibrational frequencies of elements paint a vivid tapestry of molecular interactions and chemical bonds. Through techniques like infrared and Raman spectroscopy, scientists unravel the intricate dance of atoms within crystal lattices, offering glimpses into the hidden realms of molecular structure and energy exchange.

For a deeper exploration of this fascinating topic, readers are encouraged to refer to my earlier book, 'Consciousness: The Power of Vibration and Frequency.'

* * *

As WE VENTURE further into the essence of crystals, we unveil a realm where the boundaries between the physical and the metaphysical blur—a domain where ancient wisdom and modern science intertwine seamlessly. Crystals serve as vital companions on our voyage of spiritual and energetic discovery.

CRYSTAL IDENTIFICATION AND SELECTION

Identifying and selecting crystals is an essential aspect of working with these powerful tools for healing and spiritual growth. Here are some guidelines to help you navigate the vast array of crystals available:

- **Research and Education:** Begin by educating yourself about different types of crystals, their properties, and meanings. There are numerous books, websites, and courses available that provide valuable information on crystal identification and metaphysical properties. Familiarise yourself with the characteristics of popular crystals and their associated chakras, elements, and healing properties.

- **Observation and Intuition:** When selecting crystals, trust your intuition and pay attention to how you feel when interacting with them. Take time to observe the colours, shapes, textures, and energy vibrations of each crystal. Notice which ones resonate with you on a deep level and evoke feelings of peace, harmony, or excitement. Your intuition is a valuable tool for choosing crystals that align with your intentions and energy.

- **Physical Characteristics:** Learn to identify different types of crystals based on their physical characteristics such as colour, transparency, hardness, and crystal structure. For example, quartz crystals are typically clear or translucent with a hexagonal shape, while amethyst crystals are purple and may contain visible inclusions or banding patterns.

- **Metaphysical Properties:** Consider the metaphysical properties and healing qualities associated with each crystal. For instance, amethyst is often used for spiritual protection, intuition, and stress relief, while rose quartz is known for promoting love, compassion, and emotional healing. Choose crystals that resonate with your specific goals, intentions, and areas of healing or personal growth.

- **Cleansing and Programming:** Once you've selected your crystals, it's essential to cleanse them of any negative energies and program them with your intentions. You can cleanse crystals using various methods such as smudging with sage or palo santo, bathing them in sunlight or moonlight, or placing them in a bowl of saltwater. To program your crystals, hold them in your hands, clear your mind, and focus on your intention for using the crystal. Visualise your intention being infused into the crystal's energy field.

ETHICAL SOURCING AND SUSTAINABILITY

In recent years, there has been growing awareness and concern about the ethical and environmental issues associated with the mining and trade of crystals. As conscious consumers, it's essential to consider the ethical sourcing and sustainability of the crystals we purchase. Here are some key considerations:

- **Fair Trade Practices:** Look for crystal suppliers and retailers that adhere to fair trade principles and support ethical labor practices. Fair trade ensures that miners and workers receive fair wages, safe working conditions, and opportunities for economic empowerment. By purchasing ethically sourced crystals, you can support communities and artisans around the world while promoting social justice and human rights.

- **Responsible Mining:** Choose crystals that are sourced from mines that prioritise environmental sustainability and responsible mining practices. Responsible mining involves minimising environmental impact, protecting ecosystems and wildlife habitats, and reclamation of mined areas. Look for certifications or assurances from suppliers that their crystals are mined ethically and sustainably.

- **Transparency and Traceability:** Seek out crystal suppliers that provide transparent information about the origins of their crystals and the supply chain process. Look for suppliers who can trace the journey of the crystals from the mine to the market and provide details about mining practices, labor conditions, and environmental impact assessments. Transparency helps build trust and accountability within the crystal industry and allows consumers to make informed choices about the crystals they purchase.

- **Support Local and Artisanal Sources:** Consider purchasing crystals from local artisans, small-scale miners, or independent crystal shops that prioritise ethical sourcing and sustainability. Supporting local and artisanal businesses not only ensures that you're getting high-quality crystals but also contributes to the local economy and community development.

- **Sustainable Practices:** Practice mindfulness and sustainability in how you use and care for your crystals. Avoid excessive consumption and hoarding of crystals, and instead focus on building a meaningful and intentional collection. Reuse and repurpose crystals whenever possible, and consider sharing or gifting crystals that are no longer serving you. By adopting sustainable practices, we can minimise our environmental footprint and contribute to the preservation of the Earth's natural resources for future generations.

IN CONCLUDING our exploration of crystals, we emphasise the importance of understanding and connecting with these potent allies on our spiritual journey. By learning to identify and choose crystals aligned with our intentions, we unlock their transformative power for healing and growth. This foundation not only deepens our connection with crystals but also prepares us for the forthcoming exploration of chakra evolution. As we delve into chakra healing and spiritual growth, let us carry forward the wisdom gained from our crystal connection, allowing it to inspire and guide us toward enlightenment and self-discovery.

PHASE ONE - CHAKRA - AWAKENING AWARENESS

*W*elcome to Phase One of your journey towards becoming crystalline. In this phase, we will explore the awakening awareness of the chakra system, those subtle energy centres within your metaphysical body. As you embark on this phase, prepare to delve deeper into your energetic being and uncover the significance of each chakra's colour and its impact on your physical, emotional, and spiritual well-being.

AWAKENING AWARENESS

In the initial phase of your journey, you may encounter a heightened sense of awareness within your energetic body. Some individuals may find that certain aspects of their energy lie dormant, awaiting activation and awakening. This phase marks the beginning of that awakening process. During meditation or in the dream state, you might find yourself enveloped in a singular hue or experiencing a sequence of colours at intervals. This heightened perception signifies an awakening awareness of the chakra system, the subtle energy centres within your metaphysical body.

. . .

As you become attuned to this awareness, you can delve deeper by investigating the significance of the colours you perceive. Each colour corresponds to a specific chakra, offering insights into areas of your being that may require attention or are undergoing transformation.

LET us now explore the possible meaning of each colour and its associated chakra.

SECTION 1: RED - ROOT CHAKRA (MULADHARA)

Colour: Red
Location: The base of the spine

Physical Aspects

- Represents physical vitality, grounding, and connection to the Earth.
- Governs survival instincts, basic needs for food, shelter, and safety. It relates to the physical health and vitality of the body.

Emotional Aspects

- Provides a sense of security and stability. Feelings of safety and being rooted in one's environment. Trust in oneself and the world around.
- Supports stability in relationships and material aspects of life.

Spiritual Aspects

- Serves as the foundation for spiritual growth and connection to the physical world.
- Emphasises the importance of grounding spiritual practices in daily life. Understanding the interconnectedness of all beings and the importance of staying grounded amidst spiritual exploration.

Reflection: How can you cultivate a deeper sense of grounding and security in your life?

ORANGE - SACRAL CHAKRA (SWADHISTHANA)

Colour: Orange
Location: The lower abdomen.

Physical Aspects

- Influences reproductive health, vitality, and overall well-being.
- Regulates fluid balance and sexual function.
- Corresponds to the lower abdomen and hips.
- Governs the kidneys, bladder, and reproductive system.
- Affects the body's ability to eliminate toxins.

Emotional Aspects

- Governs our feelings, desires, and creativity.
- Influences our ability to experience pleasure and connect emotionally with others.
- Facilitates the expression of emotions freely.

- Relates to the balance of yin and yang energies, affecting emotional resilience and adaptability.

Spiritual Aspects

- Associated with our sense of abundance, pleasure, and flow.
- Connects us to divine creative energy, fostering joy, passion, and vitality.
- Enhances spiritual growth and transformation through creativity and abundance.
- Represents our connection to the deeper rhythms of nature and the universe.

Reflection: How can you tap into your creative energy to bring more passion and vitality into your life?

SECTION 3: YELLOW - SOLAR PLEXUS CHAKRA (MANIPURA)

Colour: Yellow
Location: The upper abdomen.

Physical Aspects

- Governs digestive health, metabolism, and personal power.
- Supports confidence, self-worth, and assertiveness.
- In Taoist teachings, the Solar Plexus Chakra is linked to the concept of "Qi" or vital energy

Emotional Aspects

- Cultivates self-esteem, personal power, inner strength and resilience.
- Empowers you to pursue your goals with confidence and courage.
- Imbalances may manifest as feelings of low self-worth, powerlessness, or insecurity (Judith, 2004).

Spiritual Aspects

- Represents the sense of identity, purpose, and personal power.
- Aligns with authentic self-expression and the pursuit of one's true purpose in life.

Reflection: How can you strengthen your sense of personal power and confidence in achieving your goals?

SECTION 4: GREEN - HEART CHAKRA (ANAHATA)

Colour: Green
Location: The centre of the chest.

Physical Aspects

- Associated with the physical heart, circulatory system, and thymus gland.
- Influences emotional healing, compassion, and harmony in relationships.
- Within New Age spirituality, the Heart Chakra is believed to influence the heart, lungs, chest, arms, and hands, as well as the circulatory and immune systems (Dale, 2015).

Emotional Aspects

- Governs feelings of love, empathy, gratitude, forgiveness, and acceptance.
- Supports emotional balance and connection with others.
- Affects our capacity to give and receive love, cultivate compassion, and foster harmony in relationships.

Spiritual Aspects

- Connects to higher consciousness, spiritual growth, and integration of opposites.
- Fosters unity, divine love, and integration of body, mind, and spirit.

Reflection: How can you cultivate more love and compassion in your relationships and daily interactions?

SECTION 5: BLUE - THROAT CHAKRA (VISHUDDHA)

Colour: Blue
Location: The throat area

Physical Aspects

- Linked to the throat, neck, thyroid gland, and vocal cords.
- Governs physical functions related to speech, communication, and metabolism.
- Influences the health of the throat, mouth, and vocal cords.

- Imbalances may manifest as throat infections, thyroid issues, or speech impediments according to Traditional Chinese Medicine (TCM) concepts (Valentine, 1996).

Emotional Aspects
Influences communication, self-Expression, and authenticity:

- Governs the ability to express oneself authentically and communicate effectively.
- Facilitates honest and open interactions with others.
- Supports the alignment between inner feelings and outward expression.

Supports Clear Communication and Harmonious Interactions with Others:

- Enables clear and articulate verbal expression.
- Enhances the ability to listen actively and empathetically.
- Promotes harmony and understanding in relationships.

Imbalances in this chakra may manifest as:

- Difficulties in expressing oneself openly and honestly.
- Fear of speaking up or asserting one's needs.
- Feeling unheard or misunderstood in communication.
- Emotional suppression or inhibition.
- Inability to communicate effectively or resolve conflicts.

Spiritual Aspects

- Represents truthfulness, authenticity, and alignment with one's higher purpose.
- Facilitates the expression of one's inner truth and spiritual insights.
- Acts as a bridge between the physical and spiritual realms, fostering the expression of one's true essence and spiritual insights.

Reflection: How can you express your authentic voice and communicate your truth more effectively?

SECTION 6: INDIGO - THIRD EYE CHAKRA (AJNA)

Color: Indigo
Location: The forehead between the eyebrows

Physical Aspects

- Associated with brain health, vision, and neurological function.
- Supports mental clarity, intuition, and access to higher states of consciousness.

Emotional Aspects

- Governs intuition insight, imagination
- Enhances emotional balance and intuitive clarity

Imbalances in the Third Eye Chakra may manifest as:

- Feelings of confusion
- Lack of clarity
- Difficulty in making decisions

Spiritual Aspects

- Considered the seat of higher consciousness and spiritual insight.
- Opens the doorway to spiritual awakening and expanded awareness.
- Facilitates experiences of unity and transcendence.
- Serves as the doorway to higher dimensions of consciousness and spiritual wisdom.

Reflection: How can you enhance your intuition and connect with your inner wisdom?

SECTION 7: VIOLET OR WHITE - CROWN CHAKRA (SAHASRARA)

Colour: Violet or White
Location: At the top of the head

Physical Aspects

- Associated with the pineal gland, brain, and nervous system.
- Activation enhances overall brain function and mental clarity.
- Imbalances may manifest as headaches, neurological issues, or issues with the skeletal system in Traditional Chinese Medicine (Judith, 2004).

Emotional Aspects

- Linked to feelings of unity, bliss, and spiritual ecstasy.

- Fosters inner peace, contentment, and transcendence of worldly desires.
- In Buddhism the crown chakra represents enlightenment and liberation from suffering.

Spiritual Aspects

- Considered the the seat of pure consciousness and the doorway to enlightenment and spiritual awakening.
- Facilitates unity with the divine and realisation of one's true nature.
- Promotes a sense of oneness with the universe

Reflection: How can you deepen your spiritual connection and experience a sense of oneness with the universe?

Chakra Awareness Colours - N.J. Powell

EMBRACING THE JOURNEY OF SELF-DISCOVERY

INTRODUCTION TO AWAKENING CONSCIOUSNESS

*E*mbarking on the journey of awakening consciousness marks a profound shift in perception and awareness. It's like setting sail on an ocean of self-discovery, where each wave carries us deeper into the mysteries of existence. In this chapter, we'll embark on this transformative journey together, exploring the essence of awakening consciousness, its significance in personal and spiritual development, and practical insights for navigating this voyage with grace and wisdom.

THE CALL TO AWAKENING: It is a whisper from the depths of your soul, compelling you to delve into the hidden realms of your existence. A subtle inner calling, a desire to comprehend the universe and our role within it, to explore the potential of the mind. The calling may manifest during times of crisis, loss, or disillusionment, prompting us to challenge the very essence of reality. Alternatively, it may arise from a simple sense of dissatisfaction with the world, interactions with others, and a recognition that there is more to life than meets the eye.

IT BECKONS us to embark on an inward journey, to rediscover the divine essence that lies dormant within each of us.

THE PROCESS OF AWAKENING: Like a butterfly emerging from its cocoon, the process of awakening consciousness unfolds in stages. Each stage is marked by profound insights, inner transformations, and moments of clarity and revelation. As we shed layers of conditioning, fears, and limitations, we spread our wings and soar into the boundless expanse of consciousness.

SIGNS AND SYMPTOMS OF AWAKENING

As we awaken to higher levels of consciousness, we may experience a myriad of signs and symptoms indicating that the awakening process is underway. Imagine heightened sensitivity as if the world around you becomes more vibrant and alive. Picture vivid dreams and visions guiding you on your path, and moments of timelessness where past, present, and future merge into one. Let's explore some of these signs in more detail:

- **Heightened Intuition:** Experiencing increased intuitive insights, psychic abilities, or a deeper connection to inner wisdom and guidance.

- **Physical Sensations:** Feeling tingling, buzzing, or electrical sensations in the body, particularly around the head, hands, or heart centre.

- **Time Dilation:** Perceiving changes in the perception of time, such as moments of timelessness or accelerated time.

- **Vivid Dreams and Visions:** Having vivid dreams, lucid dreams, or experiencing prophetic dreams and visions that provide insights or guidance.

- **Heightened Creativity:** Feeling inspired and creatively charged, with an increased flow of creative ideas and artistic expression.

- **Spiritual Awakening Signs:** Experiencing synchronicities, meaningful coincidences, or encounters with spiritual teachers or guides.

- **Physical Sensitivity to Energy:** Becoming more attuned to subtle energy fields or environmental toxins, leading to physical discomfort or fatigue.

- **Feeling Disconnected from Reality:** Experiencing periods of derealisation or depersonalisation, where one feels disconnected from the physical world or one's own sense of self.

- **Desire for Solitude and Reflection:** Feeling drawn to spend more time alone in introspection, meditation, or contemplation.

- **Heightened Empathy and Compassion:** Developing a deeper sense of empathy, compassion, and interconnectedness with all beings.

PRACTICES FOR CULTIVATING AWAKENING

CULTIVATING AWAKENING consciousness requires dedication and commitment to inner exploration and self-awareness. Meditation, mindfulness, yoga, breath work, and contemplative practices are like compasses guiding us through the uncharted waters of our inner landscape. By cultivating presence and awareness in everyday life, we awaken to the beauty and wonder of the present moment, anchoring ourselves in our highest truth.

GUIDED PRACTICES FOR AWAKENING CONSCIOUSNESS

Incorporating guided meditation exercises and reflective prompts can offer readers practical tools to deepen their understanding of awakening consciousness. These practices provide an opportunity for readers to engage actively with the concepts discussed in the chapter, fostering self-awareness and inner exploration. Here are some guided practices to support readers on their journey of awakening:

- **Body Scan Meditation:** Begin by finding a comfortable seated or lying position. Close your eyes and bring your attention to your breath. With each inhale and exhale, allow your awareness to move slowly through each part of your body, starting from the top of your head down to your toes. Notice any sensations, tension, or areas of ease as you scan through your body. Take your time and allow yourself to fully experience each moment of the practice.

- **Chakra Balancing Meditation:** Visualise a radiant light at the base of your spine, representing the root chakra. As you inhale, imagine this light growing brighter and more vibrant, grounding you to the earth. With each exhale, visualise any stagnant energy or tension releasing from this chakra, allowing it to flow freely. Repeat this process for each chakra, moving upward through the sacral, solar plexus, heart, throat, third eye, and crown chakras. Notice any shifts in energy or sensations as you focus on each chakra.

JOURNALING PROMPTS

TAKE some time to reflect on the insights gained from the chapter by journaling your thoughts and experiences. Consider the following prompts:

- What resonated with me most about the concept of awakening consciousness?

- How do I currently experience signs of awakening in my life?

- What challenges or obstacles am I facing on my journey of awakening, and how can I navigate them with grace and wisdom?

- What practical steps can I take to deepen my connection with my intuition and inner wisdom?

NATURE CONNECTION PRACTICE

Spend some time connecting with nature as a way to ground yourself and attune to the rhythms of the natural world. Take a mindful walk in the forest, sit by a body of water, or simply spend time in your backyard or a nearby park. Notice the sights, sounds, and sensations around you, allowing yourself to be fully present in the moment. Take a few deep breaths and feel a sense of peace and connection wash over you.

THESE GUIDED practices are intended to support you on your journey of awakening consciousness, offering you practical tools to deepen your self-awareness, connect with your intuition, and integrate the insights gained from the chapter. As you engage with these practices regularly, you can cultivate a greater sense of presence, clarity, and alignment with your true essence.

EMBRACING THE JOURNEY

Awakening consciousness is not merely a destination but rather an ongoing expedition of self-discovery, growth, and evolution. It's a sacred journey inviting us to awaken to the truth of our divine nature and to embrace life with open hearts and minds. As we navigate this voyage, guided by our inner wisdom and integrity, we become beacons of light illuminating the path for others to follow. We become catalysts for positive change in the world.

IN ESSENCE, awakening consciousness is not just a personal endeavour but a collective awakening to our interconnectedness and shared humanity. It's a call to embody the highest expressions of love, compassion, and wisdom, and to co-create a world where each being is honoured, cherished, and supported on their path to self-realisation.

HEALING TRAUMA WOUNDS AND RESTRICTIVE PATTERNS

*I*n the intricate journey of awakened awareness and self-discovery, we have courageously ventured along inner pathways, delving into the depths of our being. However, as we journey further into the recesses of the soul, we encounter aspects marked by the echoes of past wounds—trauma wounds that linger within the shadows of our energetic body, subtly shaping the contours of our existence.

THESE TRAUMA WOUNDS, though unseen, wield a profound presence within us. Nestled within the depths of our psyche, they carry the resonance of past experiences that have sculpted our emotional landscape and energetic frequency. Like silent orchestrators, these wounds influence our daily lives, mental outlook, and choices, weaving a tapestry of thoughts and emotions that shape our reality.

RECOGNISING the presence of a trauma wound often involves identifying persistent patterns of emotional distress, recurring negative thoughts or beliefs, unexplained physical symptoms, or difficulties in maintaining healthy relationships.

THE RIPPLE EFFECT OF UNRESOLVED TRAUMA

When left unaddressed, these unresolved traumas cast a shadow over our lives, manifesting as negative thought patterns, limiting beliefs, and emotional blockages. They become invisible barriers that hinder our ability to live authentically and embrace the fullness of our being. Our relationships may suffer, our self-worth may waver, and our sense of purpose may falter under the weight of these unseen wounds.

IMPACT ON CHAKRA FLOW

Trauma wounds and restrictive patterns can significantly disrupt the flow of energy through our chakras, leading to imbalances in our energetic system. When trauma is stored within the depths of our being, it can create blockages or distortions in the flow of energy, hindering the smooth circulation of vital life force throughout our chakras. These blockages may manifest as physical discomfort, emotional turmoil, or mental distress, impacting our overall well-being and sense of vitality. Additionally, restrictive patterns, such as limiting beliefs or negative thought patterns, can further impede the flow of energy, causing stagnation or depletion within specific chakras. By addressing and releasing these trauma wounds and restrictive patterns, we can restore balance and harmony to our chakra system, allowing for the free and uninhibited flow of energy throughout our being. This restoration of energetic balance not only promotes physical health and emotional stability but also supports our journey towards spiritual growth and self-realisation.

EMBRACING THE PATH OF HEALING

Yet, amidst the darkness, there is light—a beacon of hope that illuminates the path of healing and transformation. As we confront these trauma wounds and restrictive patterns, we reclaim our sovereignty and unlock the power to shape our reality. Through practices of self-inquiry, mindfulness, and compassionate self-care, we navigate the labyrinth of our inner landscape, shedding light on the shadows and integrating the fragments of our soul.

THIS JOURNEY IS NOT one of conquest or eradication but of tender self-compassion and radical self-acceptance. It is a journey of empowerment, where we acknowledge the wounds of the past not as weaknesses but as portals to profound healing and growth. With each step forward, we reclaim fragments of our essence, weaving them into the tapestry of our being with threads of resilience and wisdom.

UNDERSTANDING TRAUMA WOUNDS

Trauma wounds are not merely physical injuries; they are emotional and energetic imprints left by distressing or overwhelming experiences. These experiences can range from childhood traumas and past relationship dynamics to societal pressures and cultural conditioning. When we experience trauma, whether it be from abuse, neglect, or other forms of adversity, our energetic body absorbs the shock and stores it within our cellular memory. These wounds, stored within the depths of our being, hold the frequency of past experiences, shaping our emotional landscape and energetic resonance. This stored energy can manifest as chronic stress, anxiety, depression, and a sense of disconnection from ourselves and others. They can manifest as negative thought patterns, limiting beliefs, and emotional blockages that hinder our ability to live fully and authentically.

EFFECTS ON DAILY LIFE AND MENTAL OUTLOOK

The presence of trauma wounds can profoundly influence our daily life and mental outlook, shaping the lens through which we perceive ourselves and the world around us. We may find ourselves ensnared in cycles of self-sabotage, repeating patterns of behaviour that perpetuate our pain and suffering. Consequently, our relationships may suffer as we struggle to authentically trust and connect with others. Additionally, the lingering effects of trauma may manifest as chronic physical ailments, as the energetic residue of past experiences creates tension and discomfort within our bodies.

TRAUMA WOUNDS, whether deeply buried or festering at the surface, exert a significant impact on our perception of reality. They possess the power to cloud our judgment, distort our understanding of ourselves and others, and influence our interpretation of events. Left unaddressed, these wounds may give rise to negative thought patterns, limiting beliefs, and self-sabotaging behaviours. Consequently, we may find ourselves trapped in cycles of fear, shame, and self-doubt, struggling to break free from the shackles of our past experiences. This can result in a lowering of our energetic frequency and the emergence of blockages within our energy body.

SHAPING REALITY AND EMBRACING GROWTH

In acknowledging our ability to shape our own reality, particularly in the aftermath of past traumas, we reclaim our sovereignty and unlock the potential to live a life aligned with our highest aspirations. Through practices like shadow work, meditation, and energy healing, we illuminate the hidden recesses of our psyche, revealing the roots of our pain and transforming them into wellsprings of wisdom and resilience.

IT'S OFTEN REITERATED that problems themselves are not inherent; rather, it's our perception of events that imbues them with the qualities of challenges or opportunities. When we view life through the filters of fear, scarcity, or victimhood, even minor setbacks can appear insurmountable. However, when we approach life with curiosity, resilience, and a growth mindset, obstacles become transformative stepping stones on the path to personal evolution.

CONSIDER THE SCENARIO: two individuals encountering identical external circumstances may respond in vastly different ways based on their internal beliefs and perspectives. What one person perceives as a catastrophic failure, another may interpret as a valuable lesson. This underscores the profound influence of mindset on shaping our reality.

BY DELIBERATELY SHIFTING our perspective and reframing challenges as opportunities for growth and learning, we reclaim our agency and resilience in the face of adversity. Rather than viewing problems as impassable barriers, we perceive them as invitations to expand our consciousness, nurture inner strength, and deepen our connections with ourselves and others.

DEALING WITH OTHER PEOPLE'S TRAUMA WOUNDS

As we navigate our healing journey, it is crucial to recognise the impact of other people's trauma wounds on our energetic field. Often, we may find ourselves entangled in the energetic residue of others' pain, absorbing their emotions and taking on their burdens as our own. However, we must remember that we have a choice in how we engage with these energies. We can choose to remain in our own energetic level, cultivating boundaries and self-care practices that protect our well-being while offering compassion and support to those in need.

TOOLS FOR HEALING TRAUMA WOUNDS

Healing trauma wounds and engaging in shadow work are integral components of the journey toward self-discovery and emotional healing. These practices require a multifaceted approach that addresses the physical, emotional, and energetic aspects of our being. Here are some helpful tools for navigating this transformative process:

- **Therapeutic Techniques:** Begin by engaging in therapy or counselling to explore and process past traumas in a safe and supportive environment.

- **Mindfulness Practices:** Incorporate mindfulness meditation, breath work, and body awareness techniques to ground yourself in the present moment and cultivate self-awareness.

- **Energy Healing:** Explore modalities such as Reiki, acupuncture, or sound healing to release energetic blockages and restore balance to your energetic body.

- **Creative Expression:** Express yourself through art, journaling, or movement to channel and release pent-up emotions and explore your inner landscape.

- **Self-Compassion and Forgiveness:** Cultivate self-compassion and self-love through daily affirmations, self-care rituals, and acts of kindness toward yourself. Additionally, practice forgiveness for yourself and others as a crucial aspect of releasing the grip of past traumas and fostering inner peace and healing.

- **Community Support:** Seek support from trusted friends, family members, or support groups who can offer empathy, validation, and encouragement on your healing journey.

SHADOW WORK: EXPLORING THE DEPTHS OF THE PSYCHE

Shadow work is a profound journey of self-discovery and integration, delving into the hidden recesses of the psyche to uncover and embrace the aspects of ourselves that we have suppressed or rejected. Through various practices and techniques, we can shine light on these shadow aspects, allowing for healing and transformation to occur.

PRACTICES USED IN SHADOW WORK:

- **Self-Reflection:** Engage in introspective practices such as journaling, contemplation, or meditation to explore our thoughts, emotions, and behaviours.

- **Exploring Childhood Experiences:** Reflect on childhood experiences, upbringing, and family dynamics to uncover patterns and conditioning that may be influencing our current behaviour.

- **Identifying Triggers:** Pay attention to situations or interactions that trigger strong emotional reactions, providing clues to underlying shadow aspects.

- **Dream Analysis:** Examine the symbolism and themes in dreams to gain insight into unconscious aspects of the psyche.

- **Creative Expression:** Utilise artistic mediums such as writing, painting, or music to express and explore unconscious emotions and themes.

- **Inner Dialogue:** Engage in internal dialogues or journaling exercises where different aspects of the self are given a voice to express their needs, fears, and desires.

- **Working with Archetypes:** Delve into the study of archetypal energies and characters that resonate with us, allowing us to gain insight into various aspects of our psyche. By exploring these universal patterns and themes, we can better understand the deep-rooted psychological and spiritual dynamics that shape our thoughts, feelings, and actions. This exploration serves as a valuable tool for navigating our personal journey of growth and self-discovery more effectively.

- **Therapeutic Techniques:** Work with therapists or counsellors trained in shadow work to facilitate the exploration and integration of unconscious material.

- **Body-Based Practices:** Use somatic practices such as breath work, body scanning, or movement to connect with and release stored emotional energy.

- **Confronting Shadow Traits:** Courageously face and accept the aspects of ourselves that we may find difficult or shameful, recognising that they are a part of the whole.

Integration and Healing:

As you engage in healing practices and shadow work, you embark on a journey of integration and transformation. By bringing the contents of your shadow into conscious awareness and cultivating self-awareness, compassion, and wholeness, you can begin to understand and accept yourself more fully. You can begin to release the grip of past traumas and step into a reality defined by joy, resilience, and authenticity. Remember, healing is a journey, not a destination, and every step forward is a testament to your strength and courage.

Empowering Perception:

By acknowledging the pivotal role that perception plays in shaping our experiences, we reclaim our power to transcend the limitations imposed by our trauma wounds. Instead of viewing challenges as insurmountable obstacles, we recognise them as opportunities for growth and self-discovery.

. . .

As we journey through the realms of healing and transformation, let us embrace every trial and tribulation as a stepping stone toward greater self-awareness and fulfilment. May we remember that our perception has the profound ability to shape our reality and manifest our highest potential.

CHANGING OUR RELATIONSHIP TO PROBLEMS

One powerful tool for shifting our perception of problems is to practice radical acceptance and non-resistance. Instead of denying the existence of challenges, we can acknowledge them with compassion and curiosity, allowing ourselves to fully experience the emotions and lessons they bring. By doing so, we release the grip of fear and attachment, opening ourselves to new possibilities and solutions.

Another effective strategy is to cultivate gratitude and appreciation for the lessons embedded within our challenges. By reframing our perspective and focusing on the blessings and growth opportunities inherent in every situation, we empower ourselves to transcend perceived limitations and co-create a reality aligned with our highest potential.

Ultimately, our perception shapes our reality. By cultivating a mindset of abundance, resilience, and possibility, we can transform problems into opportunities, setbacks into strengths, and challenges into catalysts for personal and spiritual growth. Remember, the way we perceive the world is a choice—a choice that holds the power to shape our destiny and create the life of our dreams.

THE POWER OF WORDS: TRANSFORMING NEGATIVE THOUGHT PATTERNS

Within the intricate tapestry of human experience, the words we choose and the thoughts we entertain wield profound influence over our energetic frequency and emotional well-being. Much like trauma wounds imprint themselves upon our energetic body, negative thought patterns weave themselves into the fabric of our consciousness, shaping our perception of reality and impacting the quality of our lives.

UNDERSTANDING NEGATIVE THOUGHT PATTERNS

Negative thought patterns ripple across the surface of our consciousness, emanating from the depths of our subconscious mind. These patterns often manifest as self-critical thoughts, limiting beliefs, or fear-based narratives, reinforcing feelings of unworthiness or inadequacy. Over time, if left unaddressed, these patterns become deeply ingrained within our psyche, perpetuating cycles of self-doubt, anxiety, and despair.

THE IMPACT OF WORDS ON ENERGY FREQUENCY

Words transcend mere communication; they are potent carriers of energy that can uplift or diminish our vibrational frequency. Speaking words of love, compassion, and encouragement infuses our energy field with positivity and light, creating a ripple effect that extends outward. Conversely, engaging in self-criticism, judgment, or negativity lowers our energetic vibration, fostering an atmosphere of discord and disharmony.

TOOLS FOR TRANSFORMING NEGATIVE THOUGHT
PATTERNS

Thankfully, we possess the power to transform negative thought
patterns and elevate our energetic frequency through conscious
awareness and intentional action. Here are some effective tools
and practices to help shift our relationship with our thoughts and
words:

- **Mindfulness Meditation:** Cultivate a practice of
  mindfulness to observe thoughts without attachment
  or judgment.

- **Affirmations:** Harness the power of affirmations to
  reprogram the subconscious mind with positive beliefs
  and attitudes.

- **Positive Self-Talk:** Monitor internal dialogue and
  replace self-critical thoughts with words of
  encouragement and self-compassion.

- **Creative Expression:** Express emotions and release
  negative thought patterns through art, journaling, or
  movement.

- **Energy Clearing:** Utilise techniques such as smudging
  or visualisation to cleanse the energy field of stagnant
  or discordant energies.

* * *

IN THE JOURNEY of healing and transformation, our words and
thoughts serve as both guides and barriers, shaping the terrain of

our inner world and directing the trajectory of our lives. By fostering mindfulness of our thought patterns and consciously selecting words that uplift and empower, we unlock the profound transformative power of language. As we raise our energetic frequency and cultivate a life filled with joy and fulfilment.

WE COME to realise that healing is not a destination but an ongoing voyage to ascend to higher states of consciousness. Delving into the depths of our being, we confront the scars of the past, advancing on a journey of perpetual growth and evolution. Each step forward stands as a testament to our resilience and steadfast commitment to self-discovery. Let us embrace this expedition with courage and compassion, recognising that within every moment lies the boundless potential for healing and transformation.

Visual representation of energy blockages: A pipe with blockage preventing the smooth flow of energy, causing vibrant energy to burst out in disharmony. Blockages like these can lead to disruption and imbalance in our energy system, affecting our overall well-being.

PHASE TWO - CHAKRA EARLY EXPLORATION

"The chakras are very intelligent - they are like the software of the whole computer body." - Dharma Mittra

HEIGHTENED AWARENESS

*I*n the preceding chapter, 'Healing Trauma Wounds and Restrictive Patterns,' you embarked on a transformative journey towards self-awareness and healing. Now, as you transition into Phase Two of exploring the chakras, you carry with you the profound insights gained from confronting past traumas and releasing limiting beliefs. Building upon this foundation, this chapter serves as a continuation of your exploration, guiding you towards a deeper understanding of your energetic body and its interconnectedness with your consciousness.

AS YOUR CONSCIOUSNESS EXPANDS, you naturally become more attuned to your body's signals, gravitating towards healthier lifestyle choices and self-care practices.

. . .

PRACTICES LIKE YOGA offer a path to connect with your inner self and promote physical well-being.

TIME SPENT in nature becomes a grounding experience, facilitating a reconnection with the Earth's energy and fostering inner peace.

ADDITIONALLY, incorporating moments of meditation and mindfulness into your routine provides clarity and tranquility amidst life's challenges.

YOU MAY ALSO EXPLORE the healing vibrations of sound through music or sound therapy, restoring balance and harmony within.

WITH THIS NEWFOUND INWARD FOCUS, you consciously cultivate positivity, nourishing yourself with uplifting energy and frequencies.

ENTERING INTO THE METAPHYSICAL BODY

Envision a depiction of the metaphysical body system—a human figure composed entirely of advanced yet primordial energy pipes intricately woven throughout. These pipes, crafted with a blend of ancient wisdom and futuristic technology, serve as conduits for the flow of life force energy towards chambers containing gem pools of radiant colour positioned at key energy centres along the body. Each pool symbolises a chakra, from the base to the pinnacle, pulsating with vitality and luminescence.

. . .

STARTING at the base of the figure, a rich crimson pool radiates warmth and vitality, symbolising the root chakra. Filled with a substance resembling a sparkling ruby yet liquid in form, this pool signifies the foundation of our energetic being.

CONTINUING THE JOURNEY, the intricate pipes extend, leading to an orange pool glowing with fiery energy, representing the sacral chakra. The exploration further unfolds with a golden-yellow pool exuding empowerment and willpower, signifying the solar plexus chakra. Ascending higher, a emerald green pool shimmers with powerful healing energy, symbolising the heart chakra.

THE JOURNEY then reaches a tranquil light blue pool that reflects serenity and communication, embodying the throat chakra. Continuing the ascent, you then encounter an indigo pool resonates with intuition and insight, representing the third eye chakra. At the pinnacle of the figure's form, a pool of gentle rose quartz-coloured liquid radiates unconditional love and divine connection, symbolising the crown chakra.

EACH POOL IS FILLED with a thick, luminescent liquid, reminiscent of liquid crystal, pulsating with energy and vitality.

THE ENTIRE SCENE is bathed in a soft, ethereal glow, casting shadows that dance and shift with the ebb and flow of energy. This depiction captures the intricate interconnectedness of the metaphysical body system in early development, illustrating the harmonious balance and alignment of chakras as they channel and distribute universal life force energy.

* * *

ROOT CHAKRA IN EARLY DEVELOPMENT

Illustration description

At the centre of the image stands a gem pool of vibrant ruby-red energy symbolising the root chakra. Filled with a thick, luminescent liquid crystal, shimmering with intense sparkling ruby-red hues. This pool represents the foundational energy centre associated with grounding, stability, and survival.

. . .

CONVERGING TOWARD THE RUBY-RED POOL, energy pipes adorned with intricate engravings and symbols channel energy from all directions, blending ancient wisdom with futuristic technology.

BATHED IN A WARM, pulsating glow, the scene evokes a sense of ancient power and cosmic connection, inviting contemplation of the profound mysteries of the metaphysical realm.

Passing through chambers adorned with shimmering crystal pools of vibrant energy, the journey culminates in the ethereal beauty of the Rose Quartz chamber.

PHASE THREE - CHAKRA DEVELOPMENTS

"The heart chakra is the centre of transformation that bridges the gap between our human and soul form. It is the place where the physical and spiritual meet." - Anodea Judith

*I*n phase three of our exploration into chakra development, we delve deeper into the transformative journey of our energetic centres. Transitioning from our previous phase, where we focused on understanding and nurturing our chakras, phase three represents a significant milestone in our quest for self-awareness and spiritual growth.

HERE, we delve into how the evolution of our chakras mirrors the grand narrative of cosmic creation, intricately weaving together threads of interconnectedness and harmony. Each stage of chakra development reflects a different facet of the universe's formation, guiding us towards a greater self-awareness, harmony, and deeper understanding of ourselves and our connection to the cosmos.

. . .

JOIN me as we unravel the profound significance of phase three chakra developments in our pursuit of enlightenment.

PHASE THREE - CHAKRA DEVELOPMENTS

The transformation of chakra liquid crystal pools into landscapes of crystals and minerals serves as a profound testament to the intricate interplay between the physical and metaphysical realms. This transition mirrors the fascinating phenomenon observed in the physical world, where liquid crystals can undergo phase transitions into crystalline structures under specific conditions. (Collings, 1990).

AS CRYSTALS FORM, they unveil intricate geometric patterns and symmetries, embodying principles of harmony and balance found in nature. These crystalline structures provide stable environments for the intricate biochemical reactions necessary for life to flourish, laying the groundwork upon which life emerges and thrives. Essentially, the transition from liquid crystal to crystal formation represents a pivotal step in the emergence of life itself, emphasizing the profound interconnectedness between the physical world and the origins of life.

AS WE MARVEL at the dualities present in chakra development and the physical world, we recognise a mirrored reflection of order emerging from chaos and coherence arising from fluidity. From the genesis of life to the evolution of consciousness, our journey is marked by a continuous dance between form and formlessness, structure and fluidity. As our chakras evolve, they serve as a microcosm of this cosmic dance, guiding us towards greater self-awareness, harmony, and unity with the universe.

*Root Chakra (Muladhara) Development - Obsidian cliffs with red liquid crystal
(Possibly magma)*

Root Chakra (Muladhara) - Obsidian Cliffs with Red Liquid

Here, the liquid pool of crystal energy has metamorphosed into a landscape of obsidian cliffs, with red liquid broiling with energy, closely embodying the essence of the root chakra. This imagery symbolises the grounding and foundational energy that anchors us to the physical realm, reflecting the core attributes of the root chakra. Just as the Earth's core harbours both molten magma and solid rock, embodying the duality of stability and transformation, so too does the root chakra embody the balance between stability and change within our energetic being.

Sacral Chakra (Swadhisthana) - Suspended molten golden substance

SACRAL CHAKRA (SWADHISTHANA) - Suspended Molten Golden Substance

Ascending further, we encounter a mesmerising sight: the once fiery orange pool has transformed into a molten golden substance suspended in the chamber. Elemental particles coalesce, creating undulating waves in this malleable form of creation. This molten essence symbolises the sacral chakra, embodying the dynamic interplay of elemental forces and reflecting the boundless potential for creativity and transformation inherent to this chakra.

Solar Plexus Chakra (Manipura) - Glowing bright like the sun

SOLAR PLEXUS CHAKRA (Manipura) - Bright Sun-like Glow

Stepping into the luminous warmth of the yellow chamber, we encounter a vibrant depiction of the solar plexus chakra, glowing bright like the sun. This radiant imagery symbolises the fiery energy of willpower and self-confidence, reminiscent of the sun's radiance and warmth. Much like the sun's vital role in sustaining life on Earth, the solar plexus chakra serves as a powerhouse within our energy body, influencing our digestive health, metabolism, and overall vitality. Much like the sun's illumination of the world, the solar plexus chakra enables us to express our true essence, radiating our unique light and making a positive impact on the world around us.

Heart Chakra (Anahata) - Emerald woods

Heart Chakra (Anahata) - Emerald Woods

The depiction of emerald woods encapsulates the heart chakra's essence, symbolising nature's nurturing and compassionate energy. Teeming with trees that oxygenate the air essential for life, the landscape mirrors how love serves as the vital force powering higher energetic frequencies. The emerald woods represent the heart chakra's essence, reflecting nature's nurturing energy and interconnectedness, while also influencing emotional healing, physical well-being, and spiritual growth.

Throat Chakra (Vishuddha) - Blue sky

THROAT CHAKRA (VISHUDDHA) - **Blue Sky**

The image of the blue sky perfectly corresponds to the description of the throat chakra, embodying the expansive energy of communication and expression. It mirrors the vastness and clarity of the heavens above, echoing the essence of the throat chakra. Just as the boundless expanse of the sky allows for openness and freedom, the throat chakra facilitates honest and open interactions with others. It acts as a bridge between the physical and spiritual realms, fostering the expression of one's true essence and spiritual insights, much like the sky serves as a bridge between life on earth and the boundless expanse of space.

Third Eye Chakra (Ajna) - Space

THIRD EYE CHAKRA (Ajna) - Space

This image symbolises the third eye chakra, represented by space. It signifies the boundless realm of intuition and insight, inviting us to transcend the limitations of physical perception and tap into higher states of consciousness. Much like space offers an unexplored frontier of endless possibilities, the change of perception obtained by unveiling the third eye echoes the expansive nature of the third eye chakra and the limitless potential it holds for spiritual growth and enlightenment.

Crown Chakra (Sahasrara) - Domed Ceiling Flower design

CROWN CHAKRA (SAHASRARA) - The domed ceiling flower design correlates with the crown chakra, symbolising the pinnacle of human consciousness and connection to the divine. It transcends individuality to embrace universal oneness, reflecting the essence of the crown chakra.

* * *

CREATING A UNIVERSE WITHIN - A SUMMARY

In exploring the evolution of chakras, we uncover striking parallels with the grand narrative of cosmic creation. Each evolving chakra mirrors a different aspect of the universe's formation and development, weaving together a tapestry of cosmic harmony and interconnectedness.

PLANETARY FORMATION: The root chakra, akin to molten magma, symbolises the primal forces at play during the birth of celestial bodies. Rocks melt and meld within intense heat and pressure, shaping the foundation upon which worlds will soon stand.

STELLAR NUCLEOSYNTHESIS: The sacral chakra resonates with the alchemical dance of stellar nucleosynthesis, where elements are forged within the fiery hearts of stars, seeding the universe with the potential for life. The gilded essence of creation itself.

SOLAR SYSTEM FORMATION: As the sun takes its place at the heart of our cosmic ballet, our solar plexus chakra echoes the gravitational dance that births entire solar systems. From the swirling mists of primordial clouds, celestial bodies coalesce under the watchful gaze of the newborn sun, shaping the very fabric of space and time.

BIOLOGICAL EVOLUTION: Life, in its infinite diversity, finds its echo in the vibrant canopy of our heart chakra, where the emerald embrace of nature gives rise to the symphony of existence. Like the towering sentinels of the forest, trees stand as silent witnesses to the eons-long saga of biological evolution, their roots reaching deep into the fertile soil of creation.

. . .

ATMOSPHERIC COMPOSITION: Above, beneath the azure canvas of the sky, the throat chakra resonates with the ethereal dance of light and air. Just as sunlight scatters across the tapestry of Earth's atmosphere, our voices echo across the vast expanse of existence, shaping the very fabric of reality with our words and intentions.

COSMOLOGICAL EVOLUTION: Beyond the confines of our terrestrial abode lies the boundless expanse of space itself, where the third eye chakra peers into the depths of eternity. Here, amidst the swirling mists of cosmic clouds, galaxies are born and die, stars blaze bright and fade, and the universe itself dances to the silent melody of creation.

TECHNOLOGICAL ADVANCEMENT: Finally, in the crucible of human ingenuity, the crown chakra reaches ever skyward, echoing the towering spires of our greatest achievements. From the humblest beginnings to the loftiest heights of human endeavour, engineering and innovation shape the course of our collective destiny, propelling us ever closer to the stars.

* * *

IN THESE COSMIC symphonies of creation, each element plays its part in the eternal dance of existence, weaving together a tapestry of life, energy, and consciousness that spans the breadth of the cosmos. Just as celestial bodies contribute to the dynamic processes shaping the universe, our chakras represent creation within ourselves.

Through this recognition, we awaken to the boundless potential within us and our role in the continual unfolding of the cosmic dance.

PHYSICAL SYMPTOMS DURING CHAKRA DEVELOPMENT

*A*s the chakras undergo development and activation, individuals may experience a range of physical changes that reflect the shifting energy within their bodies. These changes can manifest in various ways, from sensations within the body to shifts in perception and interaction with the external environment. Here, we explore some of the physical symptoms commonly associated with chakra development:

- **Sensations of Energy Flow:** As the chakras become more active, individuals may perceive sensations of energy flowing through their bodies. This can manifest as tingling, warmth, or vibrations in specific areas corresponding to the location of the chakras.

- **Changes in Physical Sensitivity:** Heightened awareness of energy may lead to increased sensitivity to physical stimuli, such as changes in temperature, pressure, or texture. Individuals may find themselves more attuned to subtle sensations in their environment and within their own bodies.

- **Altered Perception of Reality:** The activation of chakras can bring about shifts in perception, altering how individuals perceive themselves and the world around them. Colours may appear more vibrant, sounds more distinct, and emotions more palpable as awareness expands to encompass subtle nuances of existence.

- **Enhanced Intuitive Abilities:** As the chakras open and align, individuals may experience an enhancement of their intuitive faculties. This can manifest as heightened intuition, psychic insights, and a deeper connection to inner wisdom and guidance.

- **Changes in Emotional Expression:** The development of chakras can lead to a greater understanding and acceptance of emotions, resulting in shifts in emotional expression. Individuals may find themselves more in tune with their feelings and better able to express them in healthy and constructive ways.

- **Greater Sense of Grounding and Stability:** As the root chakra becomes more balanced and activated, individuals may experience a greater sense of grounding and stability in their physical bodies. This can result in increased feelings of security, resilience, and connection to the Earth.

- **Alignment with Purpose and Authenticity:** As the chakras come into alignment, individuals may feel a deepening sense of alignment with their life's purpose and authenticity. This can lead to a greater clarity of vision, enhanced creativity, and a stronger sense of empowerment in navigating life's challenges.

* * *

THE DEVELOPMENT of chakras initiates a profound journey of transformation that encompasses not only our consciousness but also our physical bodies and the world around us. By understanding the physical symptoms associated with chakra development, individuals can navigate this journey with greater awareness, resilience, and integration. As we embrace the changes that accompany chakra development, we open ourselves to a deeper experience of life and a more profound connection to the divine within and around us.

EMOTIONAL CLEANSING AND PHYSICAL SYMPTOMS DURING CHAKRA DEVELOPMENT

In the journey of spiritual evolution, the development of chakras initiates not only a profound transformation in consciousness but also in the physical body and the world around us. As individuals embark on this transformative path, they may encounter various physical symptoms and signs indicating the process of chakra development unfolding within them.

AS THE ENERGY begins to flow through the body, it can sometimes bring up past trauma stored in the body, negative patterns, or low-vibration energies that are holding us back. This shift in frequency within our bodies can manifest as what is commonly referred to as "ascension flu."

SIMILAR TO HOW the body fights off infection and experiences symptoms as it heals, the metaphysical "infections" in our energy system may require a period of healing, adjustment, and realignment. During this period, it is essential to stay hydrated, practice self-love, and engage in grounding practices to support the body's natural healing process.

ADDITIONALLY, it's crucial to ensure that there aren't any underlying physical health issues contributing to these symptoms. Consulting with a healthcare professional, such as your general practitioner, can provide reassurance and address any concerns regarding your physical well-being.

LET'S delve deeper into understanding both the physical symptoms and ascension flu symptoms commonly experienced during chakra development:

ASCENSION FLU SYMPTOMS

Ascension flu symptoms can vary widely among individuals and may include:

- **Fatigue and Lethargy:** Feeling unusually tired or exhausted, despite getting adequate rest.

- **Headaches and Migraines:** Experiencing frequent headaches or migraines, often accompanied by pressure or discomfort in the head.

- **Body Aches and Pains:** Sensing general body aches, muscle soreness, or joint pain without a clear physical cause.

- **Digestive Issues:** Experiencing digestive disturbances such as bloating, gas, diarrhoea, or constipation.

- **Flu-Like Symptoms:** Feeling feverish, chills, or experiencing flu-like symptoms such as body aches, sore throat, and nasal congestion.

- **Emotional Upheaval:** Undergoing periods of intense emotions, mood swings, or emotional sensitivity, often without a clear external trigger.

- **Sleep Disturbances:** Experiencing changes in sleep patterns, including difficulty falling asleep, waking up frequently during the night, or experiencing vivid dreams.

- **Heightened Sensitivity:** Becoming more sensitive to energy, emotions, and external stimuli, leading to feelings of overwhelm or sensory overload.

- **Heightened Intuition:** Experiencing increased intuitive insights, psychic abilities, or a deeper connection to inner wisdom and guidance.

- **Physical Sensations:** Feeling tingling, buzzing, or electrical sensations in the body, particularly around the head, hands, or heart centre.

- **Time Dilation:** Perceiving changes in the perception of time, such as moments of timelessness or accelerated time.

- **Vivid Dreams and Visions:** Having vivid dreams, lucid dreams, or experiencing prophetic dreams and visions that provide insights or guidance.

- **Heightened Creativity:** Feeling inspired and creatively charged, with an increased flow of creative ideas and artistic expression.

- **Spiritual Awakening Signs:** Experiencing synchronicities, meaningful coincidences, or encounters with spiritual teachers or guides.

- **Physical Sensitivity to Energy:** Becoming more attuned to subtle energy fields or environmental toxins, leading to physical discomfort or fatigue.

- **Feeling Disconnected from Reality:** Experiencing periods of derealisation or depersonalisation, where one feels disconnected from the physical world or one's sense of self.

- **Desire for Solitude and Reflection:** Feeling drawn to spend more time alone in introspection, meditation, or contemplation.

- **Heightened Empathy and Compassion:** Developing a deeper sense of empathy, compassion, and interconnectedness with all beings.

While these symptoms can be challenging to navigate, they are often viewed within spiritual communities as signs of growth, evolution, and the expansion of consciousness. It's essential to prioritise self-care during these times, including staying hydrated, getting adequate rest, engaging in grounding practices, and seeking support from spiritual or holistic practitioners if needed. Remember to be compassionate to yourself and others as you navigate this transformative journey.

WAYS TO IMPROVE THE FREQUENCY IN YOUR HOME AND LIFE

Creating a harmonious and high-frequency environment in your home and life is paramount to supporting your journey of spiritual evolution and chakra development. Here are some practical ways to enhance the frequency in your surroundings:

HEALTHY LIFESTYLE CHOICES

- Nourishing your body with a balanced diet rich in whole foods, fruits, and vegetables serves as the foundation for physical and energetic vitality. By providing essential nutrients, you not only support your physical health but also optimise your body's energy flow, aiding in the harmonious functioning of your chakras.

- Engaging in regular exercise, yoga, or tai chi further promotes energy flow, strengthens your body, and enhances flexibility. These practices not only keep your physical body healthy but also help clear energetic blockages and maintain a smooth flow of energy throughout your energy field.

- Prioritising restful sleep, relaxation, and stress management techniques allows you to recharge and rejuvenate your energy reserves, facilitating optimal chakra alignment and spiritual growth.

Nature Connection

- Spending time in nature regularly offers a profound opportunity to recharge and align with the natural rhythms of the Earth. Nature has a remarkable ability to cleanse and revitalise our energy, helping to restore balance and harmony within our chakra system.

- Bringing elements of nature into your home, such as plants, flowers, and natural materials, infuses your space with vitality and grounding energy. This connection to nature not only enhances the frequency of your environment but also fosters a deeper sense of peace and well-being within you.

- Practicing earthing by walking barefoot on the grass or soil allows you to connect directly with the Earth's healing energy, promoting physical, emotional, and spiritual alignment.

Clearing and Cleansing Rituals

- Regularly smudging your home with sage, palo santo, or other cleansing herbs serves as a powerful method to clear out stagnant energy and negativity, creating space for positive vibrations to thrive.

- Sound healing tools, such as singing bowls, bells, or tuning forks, have the ability to break up dense energy and raise the vibrational frequency of your space, promoting healing and balance within your chakra system.

- Opening windows and allowing fresh air and natural light to flow into your home revitalises the space, promoting a sense of renewal and vitality.

Crystals and Gemstones

- Utilising crystals and gemstones strategically placed around your home amplifies positive energy and balances the chakras, enhancing spiritual growth and emotional well-being.

- Regularly cleansing and charging your crystals under the light of the full moon or with sunlight keeps them energetically vibrant, ensuring their continued support in your chakra development journey.

- Crystals such as clear quartz, amethyst, rose quartz, and citrine known for their cleansing, healing, and energising properties.

Energy Healing Practices

- Incorporating energy healing modalities, such as Reiki, acupuncture, or pranic healing, into your self-care routine helps to balance and harmonise your energy field, facilitating optimal chakra alignment and spiritual growth.

- Mindfulness meditation cultivates inner peace, clarity, and presence, allowing higher frequencies to flow through your being and supporting the harmonious functioning of your chakras.

- Breath-work techniques, such as pranayama or conscious breathing, cleanse and energise your body, mind, and spirit, promoting optimal chakra alignment and spiritual growth.

Intention Setting and Visualisation

- Setting clear intentions for the energy you wish to cultivate in your home and life focuses your energy and accelerates your spiritual growth.

- Visualizing your home filled with radiant light and positive energy invites in blessings, protection, and healing vibrations, supporting optimal chakra alignment and spiritual well-being.

- Using affirmations and positive affirmations reinforces your intentions and shifts your mindset towards positivity and empowerment, facilitating the manifestation of your desires and enhancing your spiritual growth journey.

BY INCORPORATING these practices into your daily life, you create a supportive and uplifting environment that fosters spiritual growth, emotional well-being, and vibrant health. Remember to tune in to your intuition and explore what resonates most deeply with you on your journey toward higher consciousness and energetic alignment.

THIRD EYE CHAKRA (AJNA)

EXPLORING THE THIRD EYE

*H*ave you ever experienced a moment of clarity so profound that it seemed to illuminate your path forward with a newfound sense of purpose and understanding? This is the essence of opening the third eye, a journey of spiritual growth and self-discovery that holds the potential to transform your perception of reality and unlock hidden dimensions of consciousness.

UNDERSTANDING THE THIRD EYE

Imagine a subtle yet powerful energy centre located in the centre of your forehead, between your eyebrows, known as the Ajna chakra or the third eye. It serves as a bridge between your physical and spiritual selves, and when it begins to open, it's as if a veil is lifted from your perception of the world. Suddenly, life becomes clearer, and your intuition becomes heightened, guiding you towards deeper insights and profound transformations. This newfound clarity can lead to significant life changes, as we may find ourselves shedding old habits and relationships that no longer align with our true path.

APPROACHING THE OPENING

But how does one approach the opening of the third eye? Is it a mystical process reserved for the chosen few, or is it something that anyone can cultivate with intention and dedication? Surrounding yourself with positive energy and seeking guidance from those who have walked the path before you can greatly facilitate the process. Additionally, ensuring that all your chakras are open and balanced is essential for the proper functioning of the third eye. It is through balance, particularly of the heart chakra, that the third eye finds its power and clarity.

METAPHYSICAL INSIGHTS

Opening the third eye grants access to universal knowledge and guidance that was previously beyond your awareness on a metaphysical level. It's like gaining access to a cosmic library filled with ancient wisdom and profound truths about the nature of reality. Through this awakening, you may gain insights into different dimensions of consciousness and existence, empowering you to navigate the complexities of your spiritual journey with greater clarity and understanding.

EVOLVING STAGES OF THE THIRD EYE

The journey of opening the third eye is not a linear process but rather a series of evolving stages, each marked by its own unique insights and challenges.

Although represented by space, the third eye has different evolutionary stages:

. . .

The Ball of Light and Transformation

- In this initial stage, the third eye appears as a ball of light, symbolising the potential for transformation and awakening within us.

The Eye is Born, a Window to the Cosmos

- As we progress, the third eye evolves into a vivid eye, symbolising our connection to the cosmos and the expansion of our consciousness. This is not an eye as we perceive in the physical world; it is a window into the cosmos.

Advanced Technology, the Window of Clarity

- In the final stage, the third eye becomes like advanced technology, offering us a clear and direct travel to higher realms of existence and understanding.

Embracing the Journey

Embarking on the journey of opening the third eye requires openness and a willingness to grow without preconceived goals. It's about surrendering to the flow of energy and allowing the process to unfold naturally. In this regard, understanding consciousness and having an awareness of the bigger picture can serve as a solid foundation for the transformative journey ahead.

* * *

PERSONAL REFLECTION

As you explore the concepts of the third eye further, I encourage you to reflect on your own experiences and feelings related to this chakra. Consider journaling your thoughts and insights, allowing yourself to delve deeper into your spiritual journey and personal growth.

Third Eye Chakra (Ajna)

PHASE 4: CHAKRAS - A STAR IS BORN

"*Your* task is not to seek for love, but merely to seek and find all the barriers within yourself that you have built against it." - Rumi

* * *

IN THE INTRICATE dance of cosmic energy, the evolution of chakras mirrors the birth of stars, each stage a testament to the awe-inspiring complexity of the universe. As consciousness expands and frequencies shift, the heart chakra emerges as the power station for the next phase of chakra evolution: Chakra Stellar Formation. In this chapter, we embark on a journey through the celestial landscape of chakra transformation, guided by the wisdom of ancient teachings and the wonder of cosmic phenomena.

Heart Chakra Powering the Chakra Transformation - N.J. Powell

CONNECTION TO COSMIC ENERGY

Chakras, the subtle energy centres within the body, are intricately connected to the cosmic forces that shape the universe. Just as stars are born from the gravitational collapse of molecular clouds, so too do chakras undergo a transformative journey, fuelled by the pulsating energy of creation. By exploring the parallels between chakra evolution and stellar formation, we gain deeper insight into the interconnectedness of all existence.

CHAKRA STELLA FORMATION

The transition from the Obsidian Landscape to a swirling vortex of energy signifies a profound metamorphosis reminiscent of a star's birth—a spectacle steeped in cosmic wonder. Much like the stages of stellar formation, the evolution of Chakra Stella unfolds through distinct phases, each imbued with captivating intricacy.

* * *

Gravitational Collapse

The vivid hues of the Chakra landscape dissipate, giving rise to molecular clouds—ethereal formations subject to the laws of gravity. These enigmatic entities contract and fragment, forming denser cores where the seeds of cosmic potential stir.

Formation of a Protostar

Deep within the heart of collapsing molecular clouds, a wondrous transformation takes shape. A protostar emerges—a radiant entity amidst the cosmic expanse, encircled by a swirling disk of gas and dust. This pivotal stage, akin to a celestial gestation, bears witness to the majestic dance of creation. (André, P. et al.; Evans II, N. J.)

Ignition of Nuclear Fusion Reactions

As the protostar matures, its core becomes a crucible of transformation. Amidst unfathomable pressures and temperatures, nuclear fusion ignites. Hydrogen fuses into helium, unleashing torrents of energy, contained within our energy system by primordial armour. In this celestial alchemy, a newborn Chakra emerges, pulsating with potential for the evolution of consciousness.

PRACTICAL APPLICATIONS OF CHAKRA EVOLUTION

THE CONCEPT of chakra evolution may initially seem abstract, yet its practical implications are profound. By consciously aligning with the energy of each chakra stage, we can actively facilitate our own personal growth and spiritual development. Through a variety of mindfulness practices, energy healing techniques, and guided meditations, we can effectively harness the transformative power inherent in chakra energy to unlock our true potential and elevate our consciousness to new heights.

PERSONAL INSIGHT: NAVIGATING CHALLENGES AND GROWTH

Personally, my journey to this point has unfolded over many years of meditative practice and shadow work. When I reached this stage, I found myself operating at a heightened frequency, experiencing phenomena like lights flickering when I entered a room, static on electronic devices, and an intense feeling of peace and happiness. Recurring number cycles appeared in my vision—222, 111, 12. My heightened intuition allowed me to confidently make strides in various areas of my life. In this state, I gained profound clarity, becoming acutely aware of aspects of my life that were not fully aligned with love.

THIS PERIOD of transformation was indeed challenging. As change began to unfold, it felt as though the ground had shifted beneath me. Although these shifts signified the greater good for all, at the time, they felt disorienting and unsettling. I encountered resistance from those whose energies did not resonate with my heightened state. However, as I continued to work on aligning my chakras and strengthening my energy field, I noticed a remarkable change. The flickering lights and disturbances on electronic devices gradually settled, replaced by a sense of stability and harmony.

As MY FREQUENCY continued to shift, I understood that some individuals were no longer in resonance with my energy. While change is often difficult and can evoke a desire to cling to what is familiar, I embraced the process with acceptance. Their departure created space for others who were aligned with my path of love and balance. While navigating these changes was not easy, I found strength in the wisdom of Ganesh, the remover of obstacles, and trusted that everything was unfolding as it should, leading me toward greater alignment and authenticity.

APPLICATIONS AND MEDITATIONS TO ASSIST CHAKRA EVOLUTION

Understanding the evolutionary journey of chakras provides invaluable insights that can be directly applied to our daily lives. This understanding fosters not only personal growth but also spiritual development and holistic well-being. By consciously aligning ourselves with the energy of each chakra stage, we can cultivate greater awareness, balance, and harmony within ourselves and our environment. Below are practical applications and exercises tailored to each phase of chakra evolution:

1. Gravitational Collapse (Root Chakra)
Practical Application: Grounding and Establishing Stability
Exercise: Practice grounding techniques such as walking barefoot on grass or soil, visualising roots extending from your

feet into the Earth, or engaging in activities that connect you with nature, such as gardening or hiking.

2. Formation of a Protostar (Sacral Chakra)

Practical Application: Igniting Creativity and Passion

Exercise: Explore creative outlets such as painting, writing, dancing, or playing musical instruments. Allow yourself to express your emotions freely through creative expression, tapping into the transformative power of art and self-expression.

3. Ignition of Nuclear Fusion Reactions (Solar Plexus Chakra)

Practical Application: Empowerment and Self-Confidence

Exercise: Practice affirmations and positive self-talk to boost self-esteem and cultivate a sense of personal power. Set achievable goals and celebrate your accomplishments, recognising your innate ability to manifest your desires and overcome challenges.

4. Chakra Stella Formation (Heart Chakra)

Practical Application: Cultivating Love and Compassion

Exercise: Practice acts of kindness and compassion towards yourself and others. Engage in heart-opening yoga poses, such as Camel Pose or Bridge Pose, to release emotional blockages and expand your capacity for love and empathy.

5. Advanced Technology (Throat Chakra)

Practical Application: Authentic Self-Expression and Communication

Exercise: Practice conscious communication by speaking your truth with clarity and integrity. Engage in journaling or creative writing to express your thoughts and feelings, allowing your authentic voice to emerge and be heard.

6. Intuitive Insights (Third Eye Chakra)
Practical Application: Enhancing Intuition and Inner Wisdom
Exercise: Develop your intuition through mindfulness practices such as meditation, visualisation, or intuitive journaling. Trust your inner guidance and pay attention to subtle signs and synchronicities that offer insights into your path and purpose.

7. Connection to Divine Source (Crown Chakra)
Practical Application: Surrender and Spiritual Connection
Exercise: Cultivate a daily spiritual practice that aligns with your beliefs and values, such as prayer, meditation, or contemplative reflection. Surrender to the flow of universal energy and allow yourself to connect with the divine source of all creation, experiencing a sense of oneness and unity with the cosmos.

BY INCORPORATING these practical applications and exercises into your daily life, you can align with the energy of each chakra stage, fostering personal growth, spiritual awakening, and holistic well-being. Remember to approach these practices with openness, curiosity, and self-compassion, honouring your unique journey of evolution and transformation.

Guided Meditation
To deepen our connection with the energy of each chakra stage, let us embark on a guided meditation journey.

PREPARATION

- Find a quiet and comfortable space where you won't be disturbed. Sit or lie down in a relaxed position, close your eyes, and take a few deep breaths to centre yourself. Feel the tension melting away with each exhale, allowing yourself to sink deeper into a state of tranquility.

Visualising the Cosmic Landscape

- Visualise yourself floating in the vast expanse of space, surrounded by an infinite sea of stars twinkling like diamonds in the cosmic abyss. Feel the weightlessness and expansiveness of the universe enveloping you in its embrace.

- As you gaze up at the star-filled sky, imagine a swirling vortex of energy forming around you, enveloping you in its radiant embrace. This swirling energy is the essence of your chakras, each one pulsating with its own unique frequency and colour.

Connecting with the Chakras

- Direct your attention to the base of your spine, where the root chakra resides. Visualise a vibrant red light glowing at the base of your spine, grounding you to the earth like the sturdy roots of a mighty tree.

- Feel the solidity and stability of the earth beneath you, supporting and nourishing you as you embark on your journey of self-discovery. Allow yourself to connect deeply with the primal energy of the earth, feeling rooted and secure in your foundation

- Now, shift your awareness to the area just below your navel, where the sacral chakra resides. See a warm, orange light radiating from this area, igniting your creativity and passion. Allow yourself to connect with your deepest desires and emotions, embracing them with love and acceptance.

- Now, bring your awareness to the area just above your navel, where the solar plexus chakra resides. Visualise a brilliant yellow light shining brightly in this space, empowering you with confidence and strength.

- Feel a sense of courage and determination rising within you, like the blazing sun at high noon. Tap into your personal power and inner wisdom, knowing that you have the strength to overcome any challenge that comes your way.

- Now, direct your attention to the centre of your chest, where the heart chakra resides. See a beautiful green light emanating from this area, filling your heart with love and compassion. Allow yourself to open your heart fully, embracing all beings with kindness and empathy. Feel the interconnectedness of all life, knowing that love is the essence of existence.

- Moving upwards, focus on the throat chakra, located at the base of your throat. Visualise a soothing blue light shining in this space, enabling you to express yourself freely and authentically. Feel the energy of communication flowing through you, connecting you with others in a profound and meaningful way. Allow your voice to be heard, knowing that your words have the power to create positive change in the world.

- Now, bring your attention to the area between your eyebrows, where the third eye chakra resides. See a deep indigo light glowing in this space, opening your inner vision and intuition. Trust your inner guidance and allow yourself to see beyond the physical realm, tapping into the wisdom of the universe. Feel your intuition guiding you along your path, illuminating the way forward with clarity and insight.

- Finally, bring your attention to the crown of your head, where the crown chakra resides. Visualise a radiant violet light beaming from this area, connecting you to the divine source of all creation. Feel a sense of oneness and unity with the cosmos, knowing that you are a beloved child of the universe. Allow yourself to bask in the glow of divine love and wisdom, knowing that you are always supported and guided on your journey.

- Take a few moments to bask in the glow of your chakras, feeling their energy flowing freely throughout your body and spirit. Know that you are a powerful being capable of creating your own reality and manifesting your deepest desires. Express gratitude for this transformative experience and the wisdom gained along the way.

- When you feel ready, slowly begin to bring your awareness back to the present moment, gently opening your eyes and taking in your surroundings. Carry the energy of this meditation with you throughout your day, knowing that you are aligned with the infinite wisdom and love of the universe.

CHAKRA EVOLUTION: UNVEILING THE COSMIC TAPESTRY OF CREATION AND CONNECTION.

In my understanding, chakra evolution embodies a profound interconnectedness with the universe, reflecting the fundamental elements present in both crystals and human beings. Crystals, composed of primordial elements formed in the cosmic crucible, serve as tangible representations of the universal creative forces. Similarly, the human body, comprised of these same elemental building blocks, resonates with the cosmic energies that flow through the chakras, our energy power centres.

IN THIS VIEW, chakras encompass not only the individual's life cycle but also echo the broader cycle of creation in the universe. Each chakra stage represents a unique facet of this interconnected journey, from the foundational energies of the root chakra to the expansive awareness of the crown chakra. Just as crystals reflect the intricate beauty of the cosmos, so too do our chakras mirror the cosmic dance of creation and evolution.

THROUGH THIS LENS, the process of chakra evolution becomes a transformative journey of self-discovery and alignment with the universal flow of energy. By recognising our inherent connection to the cosmos through our chakras, our energy power centres, we gain deeper insights into our place in the universe and our potential for growth and spiritual evolution.

POTENTIAL CHALLENGES AND PITFALLS

While the journey of chakra evolution holds the promise of profound transformation and spiritual growth, it's essential to acknowledge that it may not always be smooth sailing. Like any path of self-discovery, individuals embarking on this journey may encounter various challenges and pitfalls along the way. Here are some common obstacles and guidance on navigating them effectively:

RESISTANCE AND FEAR: As you delve deeper into chakra work, you may encounter resistance or fear arising from the subconscious mind. This resistance often stems from past traumas, limiting beliefs, or conditioned patterns that seek to maintain the status quo. When faced with resistance, practice compassion and self-love. Be gentle with yourself and explore the root causes of your fears with curiosity and openness. Techniques such as journaling, meditation, or therapy can help you uncover and release deep-seated blocks.

OVERSTIMULATION OR IMBALANCE: Intensive chakra work can sometimes lead to overstimulation or imbalance in your energy system. You may experience symptoms such as heightened sensitivity, emotional volatility, or physical discomfort. To address these challenges, prioritise self-care practices that promote balance and grounding. Engage in activities such as spending time in nature, practicing mindfulness, or receiving energy healing to recalibrate your energy field and restore equilibrium.

EGO INFLATION OR SPIRITUAL BYPASSING: In your quest for spiritual growth, beware of the pitfalls of ego inflation or spiritual bypassing. Ego inflation occurs when the ego co-opts spiritual experiences to bolster its sense of superiority or specialness. Spiritual bypassing involves using spiritual beliefs or practices to avoid addressing underlying psychological issues or emotional pain. Cultivate humility and self-awareness by staying grounded in the present moment and remaining open to constructive feedback from others. Embrace the messy and imperfect aspects of your human experience as integral parts of your spiritual journey.

UNRESOLVED TRAUMA OR SHADOW WORK: Chakra activation can bring unresolved trauma or shadow aspects of your psyche to the surface for healing and integration. While this process can be challenging, it's essential for deepening your self-awareness and fostering inner wholeness. Create a safe and supportive environment for shadow work by seeking professional guidance if needed, practicing self-compassion, and nurturing a non-judgmental attitude towards your inner wounds. Remember that healing is a nonlinear process, and it's okay to seek help when you need it.

SPIRITUAL PLATEAUS or Dark Nights of the Soul: Along the journey of chakra evolution, you may encounter periods of spiritual plateaus or dark nights of the soul—times when you feel stuck or disconnected from your spiritual path. During these periods, trust in the inherent wisdom of your soul's journey and surrender to the natural rhythms of growth and transformation. Allow yourself to rest and recharge, knowing that these phases are temporary and serve as opportunities for deeper integration and renewal.

BY ACKNOWLEDGING and addressing these potential challenges with compassion and resilience, you can navigate the journey of chakra evolution with greater clarity, grace, and authenticity. Remember that every obstacle encountered is an invitation for growth and a stepping stone towards greater self-realisation.

REFLECTION AND INTEGRATION

As we conclude this chapter on Phase 4 Chakras - A Star is Born, I invite you to take a moment to reflect on your own journey of chakra transformation. Consider the insights and revelations that have emerged as we explored the parallels between chakra evolution and the birth of stars.

TAKE some time to journal or engage in self-inquiry, allowing yourself to delve into the following questions:

PERSONAL EXPERIENCES: Reflect on your own experiences with chakra activation and evolution. How have you felt the energy of your chakras shifting and expanding over time? Are there any particular moments or practices that have had a profound impact on your journey?

INTEGRATION INTO DAILY LIFE: Consider how you can integrate the insights gained from this chapter into your spiritual practice or daily life. Are there specific mindfulness techniques, energy healing practices, or guided meditations that resonate with you? How can you incorporate these into your routine to support your ongoing growth and evolution?

CHALLENGES AND OPPORTUNITIES: Acknowledge any challenges or obstacles you may have encountered on your path of chakra transformation. How have these challenges shaped your understanding of yourself and the universe? What opportunities for growth and learning have emerged from these experiences?

. . .

INTENTIONS FOR THE FUTURE: Set intentions for how you wish to continue exploring and nurturing your chakras moving forward. What goals or aspirations do you have for your spiritual journey? How can you cultivate a deeper connection with the cosmic energies that surround and support you?

REMEMBER that self-reflection is a powerful tool for deepening your understanding and integration of the material covered in this chapter. By taking the time to explore these questions honestly and openly, you can further illuminate the path ahead and continue your journey of chakra evolution with clarity and purpose.

AS YOU NAVIGATE the complexities of the universe within and around you, may you find solace in the knowledge that you are a radiant star, shining brightly amidst the cosmic tapestry of existence.

Chakra Stella Formation - N.J. Powell

THE CROWN CHAKRA AND HIGHER REALMS OF CONSCIOUSNESS

*E*mbark on a transformative journey of spiritual enlightenment as we delve into the mysteries of the crown chakra, known as Sahasrara in Sanskrit. In Hinduism, the depiction of the crown chakra with a thousand petals symbolises the infinite nature of consciousness. The number one thousand signifies completeness and infinity, suggesting that the crown chakra encompasses all possibilities and dimensions of existence. This imagery of the thousand-petaled lotus unfolding represents the gradual expansion of consciousness towards enlightenment and unity with the divine, revealing deeper layers of spiritual insight and realisation. Like a delicate lotus flower, its thousand petals unfurl in a mesmerising dance, symbolising the boundless expanse of consciousness and our divine connection to the cosmos.

IN THIS CHAPTER, we will embark on an exploration of the symbolism and significance of the crown chakra, uncovering its transformative power in unlocking higher states of consciousness.

. . .

Historical and Cultural Context

The crown chakra holds a profound significance in various spiritual traditions across cultures and epochs. In Hinduism, it is revered as the seat of pure consciousness, representing the union of individual awareness with the universal. Buddhist teachings describe it as the point of entry to Nirvana, the state of ultimate enlightenment. Similarly, Taoist philosophy views the crown chakra as the gateway to the Tao, the underlying principle of all existence. By understanding the diverse perspectives surrounding the crown chakra, we gain insight into its multifaceted nature and its role in spiritual evolution.

ACTIVATING THE DIVINE GATEWAY

Activating the crown chakra is akin to unlocking the gates to the divine. It's believed to usher in a host of profound benefits, from heightened states of awareness to the transcendence of the ego, and a deep, soul-stirring sense of spiritual fulfilment. Imagine moments of divine inspiration cascading like gentle rain, or the steady glow of inner peace radiating from within — that's the magic of an open and aligned crown chakra.

EXPANDING CONSCIOUSNESS

As the crown chakra unfurls its petals, consciousness expands like ripples on a tranquil pond. It's a journey marked by moments of exquisite insight and revelation, leading to sustained states of unity consciousness, where the boundaries between self and other dissolve, and one perceives the interconnectedness of all beings and phenomena.

. . .

PICTURE STANDING ATOP A MOUNTAIN PEAK, the crisp, clean air filling your lungs as you gaze out at the breathtaking panorama stretching before you. That's the vista of consciousness that awaits those who embark on the journey of the crown chakra. It's a journey of discovery, of unveiling the mysteries of existence, and of embracing the interconnectedness of all life.

FUNCTION AND PURPOSE

So, what's the function of this mystical chakra? Simply put, it's the bridge between the earthly realm and the divine. It's the gateway to expanded consciousness, leading to a profound sense of unity, peace, and transcendence. One way individuals can work with the crown chakra in their spiritual practices is through meditation techniques specifically designed to activate and balance this energy centre.

BY FOCUSING attention on the crown chakra during meditation, practitioners can invite the flow of divine energy and deepen their connection to higher realms of consciousness. As we journey onward, let the crown chakra be our guiding light, illuminating the path to enlightenment and spiritual awakening.

DELVING INTO THE HIGHER CHAKRAS

As we ascend the spiritual ladder, we encounter the higher chakras — the next stage in our evolution toward higher levels of consciousness. While the traditional seven chakras are well-known, an extended system of higher chakras exists, serving as a bridge between the individual and their divine essence.

. . .

THESE ENERGY CENTRES awaken as we progress on our spiritual journey, unlocking latent spiritual potential and facilitating a profound connection with our higher selves.

ACTIVATION AND INTEGRATION

Activating the higher chakras requires dedication, inner work, and a willingness to surrender to the flow of divine energy. Practices such as meditation, energy healing, and spiritual inquiry can help unlock the latent potential of these energy centres and integrate them into our daily lives.

AS WE DEEPEN our connection with the higher chakras, we experience a profound sense of oneness with the cosmos, a deepening of spiritual wisdom, and a greater capacity for love, compassion, and creative expression.

VISUALISATION EXERCISES

Crown Chakra Activation

- Close your eyes and take a few deep breaths to centre yourself.

- Visualise a brilliant white light above your head, shimmering with radiant energy.

- Imagine this light descending gently, like a soft rain shower, until it envelops your entire body in its luminous glow.

- Feel the warmth and purity of this divine energy as it penetrates every cell of your being.

- Now, focus your attention on the crown of your head.

- Visualise a lotus flower blooming gracefully, its petals opening one by one to reveal a radiant, golden light at its centre.

- As you continue to breathe deeply, feel this light expanding and filling your entire crown chakra with its powerful energy.

- With each breath, sense the crown chakra opening wider and wider, like a blossoming flower reaching towards the sun.

- Feel a deep sense of connection to the universe and a profound awareness of your divine essence.

- Sit in this space of pure consciousness for as long as feels comfortable, basking in the glow of your activated crown chakra.

AFTER COMPLETING THIS VISUALISATION EXERCISE, take a moment to journal about any insights, sensations, or emotions you experienced during the practice. Reflect on how the activation of your crown chakra may be influencing your thoughts, feelings, and perceptions.

BY RECORDING YOUR EXPERIENCES, you can deepen your integration of the practice and gain valuable insights into your spiritual journey.

INTEGRATION PRACTICES

Practice 1: Mindful Awareness

Integrating the activation of your crown chakra into your daily life begins with cultivating mindful awareness and spiritual reflection. Take a few moments each day to pause and connect with the present moment. Notice the sensations in your body, the thoughts in your mind, and the emotions in your heart without judgment or attachment. By practicing mindful awareness, you can maintain alignment with your crown chakra and sustain higher states of consciousness throughout the day.

PRACTICE 2: Spiritual Reflection

Set aside time each day for spiritual reflection and introspection. Journaling, meditation, or contemplative walks in nature can provide opportunities to connect with your higher self and access divine wisdom. Reflect on your experiences, insights, and aspirations, allowing your crown chakra to guide you towards greater clarity, purpose, and fulfilment.

HERE ARE some specific examples of how you can incorporate these practices into their routines, making them more accessible and impactful:

MORNING RITUAL: Start your day with a few moments of mindful awareness before getting out of bed. Set an intention for the day related to activating your crown chakra and aligning yourself with higher states of consciousness. Take a few deep breaths to centre yourself and visualise a radiant white light descending from above, filling you with divine energy.

· · ·

NATURE WALKS: Take advantage of the healing power of nature by incorporating mindful awareness into your walks. Choose a peaceful setting, such as a park or forest, and pay attention to the sights, sounds, and sensations around you. Use this time for spiritual reflection, contemplating the beauty of the natural world and your connection to your crown chakra activation.

MINDFUL EATING: Transform mealtime into a sacred practice by approaching it with mindful awareness. Before eating, take a moment to express gratitude for the nourishment before you and set an intention to activate your crown chakra. Chew slowly and savour each bite, paying attention to the flavours, textures, and sensations in your body. Reflect on the interconnectedness of food, body, and spirit, allowing your crown chakra to guide you in appreciating the divine essence within nourishment.

EVENING REFLECTION: Wind down at the end of the day with a brief period of spiritual reflection. Find a quiet space where you can be alone with your thoughts. Journal about your experiences, insights, and emotions from the day, allowing your crown chakra to guide you towards greater clarity and understanding. Consider incorporating a short meditation or relaxation exercise to help release any tension or stress accumulated throughout the day and to further activate your crown chakra.

BY INTEGRATING mindful awareness and spiritual reflection into your daily routines, you can maintain alignment with your crown chakra and sustain higher states of consciousness throughout the day. Experiment with different times of day and settings to find what works best for you, and remember that consistency is key to deepening your spiritual practice.

. . .

Scientific Perspectives
Exploring Consciousness and Neuroscience
In recent years, the intersection of spirituality and neuroscience has become a focal point of research, shedding light on the physiological underpinnings of spiritual experiences. Research findings suggest that practices aimed at activating the crown chakra, such as meditation and mindfulness, can induce discernible changes in brain structure and function.

These changes often manifest as increased activity in regions associated with self-awareness, empathy, and emotional regulation. For instance, heightened activity in the prefrontal cortex, a region linked to executive function and self-awareness, has been observed during states of deep meditation and spiritual contemplation.

Furthermore, studies exploring the effects of meditation on the default mode network (DMN) of the brain have revealed notable alterations in connectivity patterns. The DMN, implicated in self-referential thinking and mind-wandering, shows decreased activity during meditation, suggesting a shift away from self-focused cognition towards a state of present-moment awareness and interconnectedness.

By summarising these key findings, we begin to bridge the gap between the metaphysical concept of the crown chakra and its tangible effects on brain activity and consciousness. This synthesis of scientific research and spiritual philosophy underscores the profound impact that practices aimed at activating the crown chakra can have on our subjective experience of reality, ultimately reaffirming its relevance in the exploration of higher realms of consciousness..

THE SPIRITUAL GATEWAY CHAKRA ALTA MAJOR

Transitioning to the exploration of the Spiritual Gateway Chakra, situated at the back of the neck, we uncover its profound significance as a conduit for receiving universal information and accessing higher dimensions of consciousness. Referred to by various names throughout history, including the 'Alta Major' Chakra and the 'Zeal Chakra', it serves as a bridge between the material and spiritual dimensions, facilitating the flow of divine wisdom, intuitive insights, and cosmic knowledge into the individual's consciousness.

ONE WAY INDIVIDUALS can work with this chakra is through practices that focus on the alignment of the spine, such as yoga or qigong, which can help activate and balance the energy flow in this region. By incorporating gentle stretches and movements that target the neck and upper back, individuals can stimulate the energy flow in the Alta Major Chakra, fostering a greater sense of connection to higher realms of consciousness.

INNER TEMPLE

Concluding our exploration, let us delve deeper into the practical aspect of aligning the crown chakra, third eye, and back of the head (Alta Major). This alignment serves as a gateway to accessing the inner temple of consciousness in spiritual practices. Through focused meditation and visualisation techniques, individuals can intentionally direct their awareness to these energy centres, fostering a harmonious flow of energy throughout the upper regions of the body.

TO ALIGN THE CROWN CHAKRA, envision a brilliant white light emanating from the top of your head, symbolising the connection to divine wisdom and universal consciousness. Simultaneously, bring attention to the space between your eyebrows, activating the third eye chakra, which governs intuition and inner vision. Finally, visualise a gentle stream of energy descending from the crown and flowing down the back of the head, aligning with the back of the neck where the Spiritual Gateway Chakra resides. This alignment creates a sacred triad, facilitating the reception of higher guidance and spiritual insights.

THROUGH REGULAR PRACTICE AND INTENTIONALITY, individuals can deepen their connection to the inner temple of consciousness, accessing profound states of awareness and communion with the divine. This alignment not only enhances spiritual experiences but also fosters inner peace, clarity of thought, and a sense of interconnectedness with all creation.

BY INTEGRATING the alignment of these energy centres into daily spiritual practices, individuals can cultivate a deeper understanding of their innermost being and unlock the limitless potential of their consciousness. As we journey onward, may we continue to explore the mysteries of existence with reverence, mindfulness, and an open heart, guided by the transformative power of the crown chakra and the higher realms of consciousness.

* * *

As we embark on our journey of self-discovery, spiritual growth, and conscious evolution, let us harness the transformative power of the crown chakra and higher realms of consciousness to guide our newly formed energy body, our 'chakra novas,' to new dimensions of conscious awareness. Through reverence, mindfulness, and intentionality, we can elevate our consciousness, deepen our connection with the divine, and embrace the infinite possibilities that lie beyond the veil of the material world. By accessing these chakras, we open ourselves to a universe of potential, expanding our understanding of reality and unlocking the secrets of our innermost being.

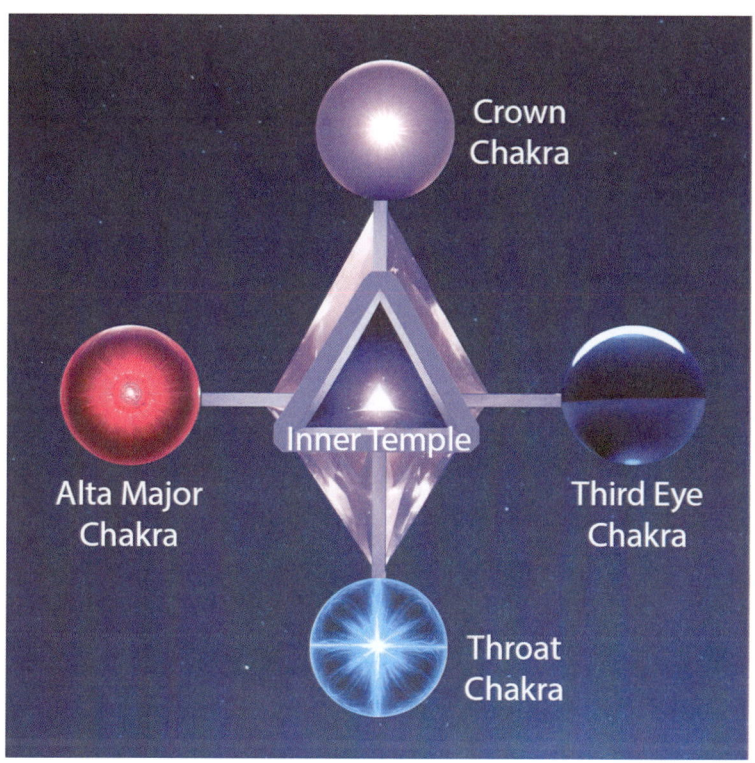

Diagram showing location of Inner Temple

BALANCING AND ALIGNING YOUR CHAKRAS - PRACTICAL EXERCISES FOR SPIRITUAL HARMONY

*E*mbarking on the path of self-discovery and spiritual awakening, we recognise the pivotal role played by the balancing and alignment of our chakras. These energy centres, in harmonious equilibrium, facilitate the unhindered flow of vital life force energy throughout our entire being, nurturing not only our physical health but also our emotional and spiritual well-being.

WITHIN THIS CHAPTER, we embark on a journey of exploration and practice, delving into the intricacies of chakra balancing and alignment. Through a comprehensive array of practical exercises and techniques, we uncover the keys to harmonising each of the seven main chakras. From meditation practices to visualisations, breath work techniques, and yoga poses, each method is meticulously tailored to activate and harmonise these vital energy centres, fostering a deeper connection with our inner selves and the universe at large.

. . .

CRYSTALS, revered for centuries for their innate ability to harness and amplify energy, serve as invaluable tools for healing, cleansing, and protecting our energy fields. When used alongside chakra balancing techniques, crystals deepen our connection with the subtle energies of the body, promoting greater harmony and well-being on all levels.

AS WE EXPLORE EACH CHAKRA, we uncover the specific crystals associated with each energy centre. These crystals possess unique vibrational frequencies that resonate with the corresponding chakras, offering targeted healing properties to clear blockages, release stagnant energy, and restore vitality to these vital energy centres.

FROM GROUNDING and stabilising the Root Chakra with stones like Red Jasper and Hematite to awakening spiritual enlightenment in the Crown Chakra with Clear Quartz and Amethyst, crystals serve as potent allies in our journey of chakra balancing and alignment.

JOIN us as we discover the transformative power of crystals and their profound synergy with chakras, unlocking the full potential of our energy system and fostering a deeper connection with our inner selves and the universe.

BALANCING AND ALIGNING PRACTICES

Root Chakra (Muladhara)

The root chakra, located at the base of the spine, governs our sense of stability, security, and survival. To balance and align the root chakra, try the following exercises:

- **Mountain Pose (Tadasana):** Stand tall with your feet hip-width apart, grounding through the soles of your feet. Visualise roots extending from your feet deep into the earth, anchoring you firmly.

- **Grounding Meditation:** Sit comfortably with your spine straight. Close your eyes and visualise a red glowing ball of light at the base of your spine. With each inhale, imagine drawing in stability and security, and with each exhale, release any fears or insecurities.

SACRAL CHAKRA (SWADHISTHANA)

The sacral chakra, located in the lower abdomen, governs our creativity, passion, and emotional well-being. To balance and align the sacral chakra, try the following exercises:

- **Hip Opening Yoga Poses:** Poses such as Butterfly Pose (Baddha Konasana) and Pigeon Pose (Eka Pada Rajakapotasana) help release tension and stagnant energy in the hips, promoting emotional flow.

- **Creative Visualisation:** Close your eyes and imagine a warm, orange light glowing in your lower abdomen. Visualise this light expanding with each breath, igniting your creativity and passion.

SOLAR PLEXUS CHAKRA (Manipura)

The solar plexus chakra, located in the upper abdomen, governs our self-esteem, confidence, and personal power. To balance and align the solar plexus chakra, try the following exercises:

- **Warrior Poses:** Poses like Warrior I (Virabhadrasana I) and Warrior II (Virabhadrasana II) build strength and confidence while promoting a sense of personal power.

- **Breath of Fire:** Sit comfortably with your spine straight. Inhale deeply through your nose, then exhale forcefully through your nose, pumping your navel in and out. Repeat this rapid, rhythmic breath for 1-3 minutes to energise the solar plexus chakra.

HEART CHAKRA (ANAHATA)

The heart chakra, located in the centre of the chest, governs our ability to love, forgive, and connect with others. To balance and align the heart chakra, try the following exercises:

- **Loving-Kindness Meditation:** Close your eyes and visualise a green light glowing in your heart centre. Send feelings of love, compassion, and forgiveness to yourself and others, expanding this loving energy out into the world.

- **Heart-Opening Yoga Poses:** Poses such as Camel Pose (Ustrasana) and Bridge Pose (Setu Bandhasana) open the chest and heart centre, releasing tension and promoting feelings of love and compassion.

THROAT CHAKRA (VISHUDDHA)

The throat chakra, located in the throat region, governs our communication, self-expression, and authenticity. To balance and align the throat chakra, try the following exercises:

- **Lion's Breath:** Sit comfortably with your spine straight. Inhale deeply through your nose, then exhale forcefully through your mouth while sticking out your tongue and roaring like a lion. Repeat this breath 3-5 times to release tension and stimulate the throat chakra.

- **Expressive Journaling:** Write freely without judgment, allowing your thoughts and feelings to flow onto the page. This practice helps unlock authentic self-expression and clears blockages in the throat chakra.

THIRD EYE CHAKRA (Ajna)

The third eye chakra, located between the eyebrows, governs our intuition, insight, and inner wisdom. To balance and align the third eye chakra, try the following exercises:

- **Third Eye Meditation:** Close your eyes and focus your attention on the space between your eyebrows. Imagine a deep, indigo-blue light glowing at this point, activating your intuition and inner vision.

- **Alternate Nostril Breathing:** Sit comfortably with your spine straight. Use your right thumb to close your right nostril and inhale deeply through your left nostril. Then, close your left nostril with your ring finger and exhale through your right nostril. Continue alternating nostrils for several rounds to balance the left and right hemispheres of the brain and awaken the third eye.

Crown Chakra (Sahasrara)

The crown chakra, located at the top of the head, governs our connection to the divine, spiritual enlightenment, and universal consciousness. To balance and align the crown chakra, try the following exercises:

- **Crown Chakra Meditation:** Sit comfortably with your spine straight. Close your eyes and visualise a brilliant white or violet light radiating from the top of your head, connecting you to the cosmos and divine wisdom.

- **Sahaja Yoga Meditation:** Practice Sahaja Yoga, a meditation technique that aims to awaken the dormant Kundalini energy and achieve self-realisation. This technique involves clearing the chakras and allowing the Kundalini energy to rise naturally through the crown chakra.

INTEGRATION PRACTICES

- **Mindful Awareness:** Take a few moments each day to pause and connect with the present moment. Notice the sensations in your body, the thoughts in your mind, and the emotions in your heart without judgment or attachment.

- **Spiritual Reflection:** Set aside time each day for spiritual reflection and introspection. Journaling, meditation, or contemplative walks in nature can provide opportunities to connect with your higher self and access divine wisdom.

USING CRYSTALS TO HEAL, CLEANSE AND PROTECT CHAKRAS

Let's delve into the profound synergy between crystals and chakras, uncovering their potential for deep healing, energetic cleansing, and spiritual protection. For centuries, crystals have been revered for their innate ability to harness and amplify energy, making them invaluable tools for chakra balancing and alignment. By incorporating specific crystals into your spiritual practice, you can enhance the flow of energy within your chakras, promote emotional well-being, and strengthen your overall energetic vitality.

HEALING CRYSTALS for Each Chakra

- **Root Chakra (Muladhara):** To ground and stabilise the Root Chakra, consider working with crystals such as Red Jasper, Hematite, and Smoky Quartz. These stones provide a sense of security, helping to anchor your energy to the earth and foster a deep sense of stability.

- **Sacral Chakra (Svadhisthana):** To ignite creativity and passion within the Sacral Chakra, opt for crystals like Carnelian, Orange Calcite, and Sunstone. These vibrant stones stimulate the flow of creative energy, enhance emotional balance, and ignite a sense of joy and vitality.

- **Solar Plexus Chakra (Manipura):** For empowerment and confidence in the Solar Plexus Chakra, choose crystals such as Citrine, Yellow Jasper, and Tigers Eye. These stones radiate warmth and strength, boosting self-esteem and personal power.

- **Heart Chakra (Anahata):** To open and heal the Heart Chakra, consider working with crystals like Rose Quartz, Green Aventurine, and Rhodonite. These gentle stones foster compassion, forgiveness, and unconditional love, promoting harmony in relationships and inner peace.

- **Throat Chakra (Vishuddha):** To enhance communication and self-expression, opt for crystals such as Aquamarine, Blue Lace Agate, and Lapis Lazuli. These soothing stones facilitate clear and authentic communication.

- **Third Eye Chakra (Ajna):** For intuition and insight, choose crystals like Amethyst, Fluorite, and Sodalite. These visionary stones heighten psychic awareness and deepen connection to higher wisdom.

- **Crown Chakra (Sahasrara):** To awaken spiritual enlightenment and divine connection in the Crown Chakra, consider working with crystals such as Clear Quartz, Amethyst, and Selenite. These powerful stones elevate consciousness, purify the energy field, and facilitate a profound connection to the divine.

Cleansing and Protecting Your Energy

In addition to healing specific chakras, crystals can cleanse and protect your energy field, ensuring clarity and vibrancy in your spiritual practice. Some crystals excel at absorbing negative energy and purifying the aura, while others create a protective shield against unwanted influences, promoting energetic harmony.

TO CLEANSE YOUR ENERGY FIELD, consider using crystals such as Black Tourmaline, Smoky Quartz, and Selenite. These stones have a potent cleansing effect, absorbing and transmuting negative energy into light. You can place them around your home or workspace, wear them as jewellery, or hold them in your hands during meditation to purify your energy field and restore balance.

TO PROTECT **your energy from external influences**, consider working with crystals like Amethyst, Labradorite, and Black Obsidian. These stones create a protective barrier around your aura, shielding you from psychic attacks, negative vibrations, and energetic vampires. Carry them with you or place them in your environment to create a sacred space of energetic protection and harmony.

STRENGTHENING OVERALL ENERGY

Incorporating crystal energy into your chakra balancing routine can amplify the process and deepen spiritual harmony. Each crystal resonates with specific chakras, offering targeted healing properties to clear blockages and restore vitality to energy centres.

Experiment with different crystals, trust your intuition, and allow the transformative energy of these sacred stones to guide you on your path to spiritual awakening and enlightenment.

* * *

INCORPORATING these practical exercises into your daily routine can help you balance and align your chakras, promoting harmony and well-being on all levels of your being. Experiment with different techniques and listen to your body's wisdom as you embark on this journey of self-discovery and spiritual growth. By combining practical exercises with the potent energy of crystals, you can create a holistic approach to chakra balancing that nurtures your body, mind, and spirit, fostering a deeper sense of harmony and well-being.

REMEMBER, the path to chakra balance is unique to each individual, so honour your own process and trust in the transformative power of your inner light.

Diagram to illustrate Chakra alignment

GUIDANCE ON ENERGY
PROTECTION AND GROUNDING

*a*s we embark on the journey of chakra work and delve deeper into the exploration of our inner realms, it becomes essential to cultivate practices for protecting our energy fields and grounding ourselves. Building upon the foundational understanding of chakras established in the preceding chapters, this chapter delves into the practical aspects of energy protection and grounding. Here, we will explore techniques and guidance to shield our energetic boundaries, clear negative energies, and maintain a grounded presence in our everyday lives. By incorporating these practices, we empower ourselves to navigate the spiritual realms with confidence and clarity.

A call to you the Reader,

Engagement from you is paramount in making the concepts of energy protection and grounding more relatable and actionable. Throughout this chapter, I'll incorporate questions, prompts, and reflective exercises to invite you to actively participate in your spiritual journey.

As we explore various grounding techniques, take this opportunity to immerse yourself in the practice. After each technique, I encourage you to pause, try it out immediately, and reflect on your experience. Notice any shifts in your energy, emotions, or state of mind. Consider journaling your observations to deepen your understanding and track your progress over time.

For example, after discussing the barefoot walking technique, you might step outside, kick off your shoes, and take a few mindful steps on the grass or soil. Pay attention to the sensations beneath your feet, the connection with the Earth, and any changes in your awareness. Then, take a moment to journal about your experience, noting any insights or feelings that arise.

By actively engaging with these practices, you not only deepen your understanding but also integrate them more fully into your daily life. Remember, your journey of spiritual growth is unique, and these exercises are meant to support and enhance your personal exploration.

Now, let's embark on this journey together, with open hearts and receptive minds, as we discover the transformative power of energy protection and grounding.

SETTING ENERGETIC BOUNDARIES

ESTABLISHING clear boundaries is fundamental to protecting our energy fields from external influences and maintaining our emotional and spiritual well-being. It is important to understand why establishing boundaries is crucial. Porous boundaries can lead to energy depletion, empathic overload, and difficulty in maintaining personal autonomy.

ENERGY PROTECTION AND GROUNDING PRACTICES

With a solid understanding of the significance of boundaries, let's explore practical techniques for energy protection and grounding. These essential practices are crucial for maintaining balance and harmony in our energetic bodies. As we navigate the intricacies of the spiritual realm, we encounter various energies that can affect our well-being. By incorporating these practices into our daily lives, we can shield ourselves from external influences and maintain a strong connection to the Earth's grounding energies. Additionally, we will delve into the concept of energy vortex protection, a powerful technique for safeguarding our energy fields from unwanted intrusions and disturbances. Through these practices, we empower ourselves to navigate the energetic landscape with confidence and resilience, fostering a deeper sense of inner peace and spiritual alignment.

TECHNIQUES FOR SETTING ENERGETIC BOUNDARIES

- **Visualisation:** Close your eyes and envision a bubble of protective light surrounding you. Intend for this bubble to act as a shield, filtering out any negative or intrusive energies while allowing positive energies to flow freely.

- **Affirmations:** Repeat empowering affirmations such as "I am safe and protected," "I honour my energy and set healthy boundaries," or "I release what does not serve me." These affirmations reinforce your intention to protect your energy field and establish boundaries.

ENERGY VORTEX PROTECTION

In addition to setting boundaries and practicing grounding techniques, harnessing the power of personal energy vortexes can be an effective method for deflecting negative energy and maintaining energetic well-being. Personal energy vortexes are like energetic whirlwinds that can be consciously created and directed to serve as shields against unwanted influences.

TO CREATE your own energy vortex for protection, follow these steps:

- **Grounding:** Begin by grounding yourself through deep breathing and mindfulness. Allow yourself to connect with your inner core and find a sense of calm and stability within.

- **Intention Setting:** Set a clear intention to create an energy vortex for protection. Visualise a swirling vortex of light surrounding you, forming a shield that repels negativity and filters out unwanted energies.

- **Visualisation:** Close your eyes and visualise the energy vortex forming around you. See it spinning rapidly, drawing in any negative or intrusive energies and transmuting them into pure, positive energy.

- **Affirmation:** Repeat empowering affirmations such as "I am surrounded by a powerful energy vortex that protects me from all harm" or "I am safe and shielded by the light of my own creation." Allow these affirmations to reinforce your intention and strengthen the energy vortex.

- **Directing the Vortex:** Once you have established your energy vortex, you can direct it to specific areas of your energy field or physical space that may need protection. Simply visualise the vortex expanding and extending its protective influence to wherever it is needed.

- **Maintenance:** Regularly reinforce and maintain your energy vortex through visualisation and intention setting. Check in with yourself regularly to ensure that your vortex remains strong and intact, and make any necessary adjustments to strengthen its protective power.

By harnessing the power of personal energy vortexes, you can create a powerful shield against negative energies and maintain a strong and resilient energetic field. Experiment with different visualisation techniques and affirmations to find what works best for you, and trust in the innate power of your own energy to provide protection and support on your spiritual journey.

Now that we've explored energy vortex protection as a powerful technique for safeguarding our energy fields, let's delve into practices for clearing negative energy and grounding. These complementary practices are essential for maintaining a balanced and healthy energy field, ensuring that we remain centred and aligned amidst the complexities of daily life.

CLEARING NEGATIVE ENERGY

Negative energy can accumulate within our energy field, affecting our mood, health, and overall well-being. It's essential to regularly cleanse and release this stagnant energy. Here are some techniques for clearing negative energy:

- **Smudging:** Burn sage, palo santo, or other cleansing herbs and allow the smoke to waft around your body and space. Visualise the smoke absorbing and transmuting any negativity into light.

- **Salt Bath:** Take a bath infused with Epsom salts or sea salt to cleanse your energy field. As you soak, visualise the saltwater washing away any negative energy, leaving you feeling purified and refreshed.

GROUNDING PRACTICES

Grounding is the process of connecting with the Earth's energy, anchoring ourselves in the present moment, and fostering a sense of stability and security. Here are some grounding techniques to incorporate into your daily routine:

- **Barefoot Walking:** Take off your shoes and walk barefoot on the grass, sand, or soil. Feel the Earth beneath your feet, and imagine roots extending from the soles of your feet deep into the Earth, grounding and stabilising you.

- **Tree Meditation:** Find a comfortable spot near a tree and sit or lean against its trunk. Close your eyes and visualise yourself merging with the tree's roots, connecting with its steady and grounding energy.

STAYING GROUNDED IN EVERYDAY LIFE

Incorporate mindfulness and awareness into your daily activities to stay grounded amidst the hustle and bustle of life. Here are some tips for staying grounded:

- **Mindful Breathing:** Take regular breaks throughout the day to practice deep, mindful breathing. Focus on the sensation of your breath entering and leaving your body, anchoring yourself in the present moment.

- **Nature Connection:** Spend time in nature regularly, whether it's taking a walk in the park, gardening, or simply sitting outdoors. Nature has a grounding effect on our energy and helps us reconnect with our essence.

THE ROLE OF CRYSTALS AND GEMSTONES

Many people use crystals and gemstones for energy protection and grounding purposes. Crystals such as black tourmaline, hematite, and smoky quartz are known for their protective and grounding properties. To select, cleanse, and use them effectively, consider the following:

- **Selection:** Choose crystals that resonate with you intuitively or research their properties to find ones that align with your intentions for protection and grounding.

- **Cleansing:** Regularly cleanse your crystals by placing them in sunlight, moonlight, or running water, or by using other cleansing methods such as smudging or sound vibrations.

- **Usage:** Carry your selected crystals with you, place them in your home or workspace, or wear them as jewellery to benefit from their protective and grounding energies throughout the day.

IMPORTANCE OF CONSISTENCY

Consistency is paramount when it comes to energy protection and grounding practices. While it may be tempting to turn to these techniques only when faced with overwhelming negativity or stress, their true efficacy lies in their integration into our daily routines. By making energy protection and grounding practices a habitual part of our lives, we create a steady foundation of resilience and stability. Consistent practice allows us to reinforce our energetic boundaries, clear away stagnant energy, and stay grounded amidst life's challenges. Just as we nourish our bodies with regular exercise and healthy eating habits, nurturing our energy field through consistent practice is essential for maintaining overall well-being. Approach these practices with dedication and commitment, understanding that the cumulative benefits of daily engagement far outweigh sporadic efforts.

OVERCOMING CHALLENGES

Navigating the journey of maintaining energetic boundaries and grounding can present various challenges, especially in the midst of stress or chaos. However, by adopting effective strategies and cultivating resilience, we can overcome common obstacles and maintain our energetic well-being with greater ease. Here are some approaches to help navigate and overcome challenges encountered on our path to energetic balance and grounding.

- **Practice Self-Compassion:** Be gentle and understanding with yourself as you navigate the challenges of maintaining energetic boundaries and grounding. Remember it's normal to face obstacles and setbacks along the way, and that self-compassion is key to overcoming these challenges with grace and resilience.

- **Cultivate Awareness:** Cultivate awareness of your thoughts, emotions, and energy levels throughout the day. By paying attention to how you feel in different situations, you can identify when your energetic boundaries are being compromised or when you're feeling ungrounded. This awareness empowers you to take proactive steps to protect your energy and ground yourself as needed.

- **Set Clear Intentions:** Set clear intentions for your energy protection and grounding practices. By clearly defining your goals and intentions, you can stay focused and motivated even when faced with obstacles or distractions. Remember that intention setting is a powerful tool for harnessing your inner strength and determination.

- **Seek Support:** Reach out for support from friends, family, or spiritual mentors when facing challenges with energetic boundaries or grounding. Having a supportive community can provide encouragement, guidance, and perspective during difficult times. Remember you don't have to navigate these challenges alone and that seeking support is a sign of strength, not weakness.

- **Practice Resilience:** Remember resilience is built through facing and overcoming challenges. View obstacles as opportunities for growth and learning rather than insurmountable barriers. Each challenge you overcome strengthens your energetic boundaries and deepens your grounding, making you more resilient in the face of future challenges.

NAVIGATING the journey of maintaining energetic boundaries and grounding can present various challenges, but it's through effective strategies and self-nurturing practices that we can overcome these obstacles and thrive. As we reflect on the importance of resilience, let's also remember the significance of self-care in fostering overall well-being and spiritual alignment.

REMINDER FOR SELF-CARE

Self-care is paramount for maintaining overall well-being, encompassing physical, emotional, and mental health. Prioritise activities that replenish your energy and nurture your holistic wellness, such as meditation, exercise, creative expression, and quality time spent with loved ones.

* * *

BY INCORPORATING these techniques for energy protection and grounding into your daily life, you empower yourself to navigate the spiritual realms with resilience and strength. Remember, these practices are not just about shielding yourself from external influences but also about cultivating a deeper connection with your inner self and the divine energies around you. As you establish healthy boundaries, clear negative energy, and stay grounded, you create a sacred space within and around you, allowing for deeper spiritual growth and transformation.

EMBRACING these practices is an ongoing journey rather than a destination. Stay open to exploration and experimentation, allowing your practice to evolve as you do. Each step you take towards greater energetic awareness and self-care contributes to your overall well-being and spiritual alignment.

IN TIMES of challenge or uncertainty, trust in the wisdom of your inner guidance and the support of the universe. You are a resilient being capable of overcoming obstacles and thriving amidst change. Honour your energy field as a sacred vessel of light, and let your journey of self-discovery and empowerment unfold with grace and authenticity.

AS YOU CONTINUE on your path, may you find solace in the grounding embrace of the Earth, strength in the protective light of your own creation, and wisdom in the depths of your soul. Embrace the journey, honour the process, and know that you are infinitely supported on your quest for spiritual growth and enlightenment.

EXPLORING SPIRITUAL DIMENSIONS

*A*s humanity delves deeper into spirituality, the concept of spiritual dimensions becomes increasingly relevant. These dimensions offer a framework for understanding consciousness, reality, and existence beyond the physical realm. Our evolving chakra system plays a crucial role in this exploration, enhancing our energy body's strength and heightening intuition as we journey through these dimensions. While interpretations of spiritual dimensions vary, a commonly referenced model includes the third dimension (3D), the fourth dimension (4D), and the fifth dimension (5D).

THREE-DIMENSIONAL EXISTENCE

In the traditional model, the third dimension (3D) represents the physical realm perceived with our senses, characterised by linear time, space, and the limitations of the ego mind, including its association with service to self.

. . .

HERE, individuals experience duality, separation, and the illusion of materiality, often perpetuated by labels, separatism, and control mechanisms. In this dimension, society operates within the confines of rules, status, and material possessions, driven by hard-working linear thinking and often led by fear. It fosters a victim mentality and perpetuates dense, slow, and heavy energy. However, as individuals awaken to higher consciousness, they transcend these constraints and explore higher dimensions.

FOUR-DIMENSIONAL EXISTENCE

The journey to 4d is a dynamic process of expansion and awakening, where individuals actively challenge old paradigms, seek deeper understanding, and align with higher purposes. In the transition to 4D existence, individuals find themselves at a mixed state gateway, where their conscious being expands its awareness and consciousness.

THEY ARE ACTIVELY CHALLENGING the old belief systems, seeking answers, and understanding the underlying structures of reality. With an increased awareness of connection, they find themselves experiencing more compassion towards others and aligning with their life's purpose. Furthermore, they adopt a more flexible approach to reality, recognising the fluidity of existence. In this state, they feel more connected to people around them and manifest their intentions and desires faster than before.

THESE TRAITS INCLUDE EXPANDED CONSCIOUSNESS, a deeper connection with subtle realms, nonlinear perception of time, and a more compassionate and purpose-aligned approach to life.

FIFTH-DIMENSIONAL EXISTENCE

The fifth dimension (5D) represents unity consciousness, where individuals transcend duality and experience profound oneness with the cosmos (Léon, 2006). Love, compassion, and harmony prevail, guiding individuals to operate from a heart-centred awareness.

TIME IS PERCEIVED as an eternal present moment, granting access to higher levels of intuition and spiritual wisdom. Associated with the awakening of higher chakras and the activation of the light body, the fifth dimension enhances one's intuitive abilities and connection to universal knowledge.

IN THIS HEIGHTENED state of consciousness, individuals align with the divine, accessing source information and receiving guidance from their spirit guides. Here, things unfold with ease and effortlessness as individuals operate from a place of light and flow, embodying authenticity and abundance. They experience a profound sense of alignment with their true essence, effortlessly embodying the qualities of love, compassion, and harmony.

ADDITIONAL DIMENSIONS BEYOND 3D, 4D, AND 5D:

In addition to the commonly referenced 3D, 4D, and 5D frameworks, various traditions propose additional dimensions beyond these, such as the sixth dimension (6D) and seventh dimension (7D), representing higher states of consciousness and cosmic awareness. Quantum physics also theorises extra spatial dimensions beyond the familiar three, essential for understanding the fundamental nature of reality (Witten, 1995).

BELIEF IN 12 DIMENSIONS OF CONSCIOUSNESS

The belief in 12 dimensions of consciousness posits a multilayered understanding of reality that extends beyond the conventional perceptions of time and space. Each dimension represents a unique vibrational frequency and level of awareness, contributing to the intricate tapestry of existence. According to this perspective, individuals progress through these dimensions as they evolve spiritually, expanding their consciousness and understanding of the universe.

WHILE THE SPECIFICS may vary among different spiritual traditions and metaphysical teachings, the concept generally suggests that higher dimensions correspond to states of greater unity, interconnectedness, and alignment with universal truths. These dimensions are often associated with qualities such as unconditional love, divine wisdom, and harmonic resonance. Proponents of this belief draw inspiration from various sources, including ancient mystical texts, channelled messages, and contemporary spiritual philosophies, to elucidate the nature of consciousness and its infinite potentiality (Hunt, 1989; Wilcock, 2011).

THROUGH EXPLORATION AND INTROSPECTION, individuals seek to transcend the limitations of the material world and ascend to higher states of being, ultimately embodying the full spectrum of their divine essence.

EMBRACING THE JOURNEY

Exploring spiritual dimensions presents individuals with a profound opportunity to broaden their comprehension of reality and transcend the limitations imposed by the ego. Practices such as meditation and energy healing serve as invaluable tools in navigating multidimensional existence and attuning to higher frequencies (Chopra, 1993). Embracing this journey and fostering the growth of our evolving chakra system not only unlocks a universe of boundless potential but also contributes to the collective evolution of consciousness.

EXPLORING SPIRITUAL DIMENSIONS THROUGH CHAKRA WORK

The journey of exploring spiritual dimensions, including the realms of 3D, 4D, and 5D, is intricately intertwined with the role of the chakra system. Each chakra serves as a gateway to different aspects of our consciousness and can facilitate access to various dimensions of existence. By understanding and working with specific chakras, individuals can enhance their experience of multidimensional reality and deepen their spiritual exploration.

ROOT CHAKRA (1st Chakra) - Connection to 3D Reality

The root chakra, located at the base of the spine, is closely associated with our physical existence and survival instincts. It serves as the foundation upon which we build our experience of the physical world, grounding us in the the present reality of 3D dimension. Strengthening and balancing the root chakra can enhance our sense of stability and security in the physical realm, providing a solid foundation for further spiritual exploration.

SACRAL CHAKRA (2nd Chakra) - Gateway to 4D Consciousness

The sacral chakra, situated in the lower abdomen, is linked to our emotions, creativity, and relationships. It serves as a bridge between the physical and astral planes, making it a vital centre for accessing 4D consciousness. By harmonising the sacral chakra, individuals can tap into the fluid and malleable aspects of the astral realm, exploring intuitive insights, and navigating the realms of dreams, emotions, and subtle energies.

SOLAR PLEXUS CHAKRA (3rd Chakra) - Empowerment in Both Realms

The solar plexus chakra, located in the upper abdomen, governs our personal power, confidence, and self-esteem. It plays a crucial role in navigating both 3D and 4D realities, empowering individuals to assert their boundaries and intentions across different dimensions. By strengthening the solar plexus chakra, individuals can cultivate the inner strength and clarity needed to navigate the complexities of multidimensional existence with confidence and resilience.

HEART CHAKRA (4th Chakra) - Pathway to 5D Unity Consciousness

The heart chakra, situated in the centre of the chest, is the seat of love, compassion, and connection. It serves as a gateway to 5D consciousness, where individuals transcend duality and experience unity with all. Activating and opening the heart chakra facilitates a deeper connection to the universal energy of love, allowing individuals to navigate the realms of higher consciousness with grace, empathy, and compassion.

THIRD EYE CHAKRA (6th Chakra) and Crown Chakra (7th Chakra) - Higher Dimensional Insights

The third eye chakra, located between the eyebrows, and the crown chakra, situated at the top of the head, are associated with

intuition, spiritual vision, and divine connection. Activation of
these higher chakras can facilitate access to transcendent states
of consciousness, including the realms of cosmic wisdom and
universal truth. By working with the third eye and crown
chakras, individuals can deepen their understanding of higher
dimensions and align with their soul's purpose within the vast
tapestry of existence.

THE INTEGRATION of chakra work with the exploration of
spiritual dimensions offers a holistic approach to spiritual
growth and enlightenment. By understanding the unique role of
each chakra and how it relates to different dimensions of reality,
individuals can embark on a profound journey of self-discovery,
transformation, and expansion of consciousness. Through
mindful exploration and cultivation of the chakra system, we
unlock the doorways to higher dimensions and embrace the infinite possibilities of the universe.

CONTEMPLATING THE NATURE OF REALITY

Exploring spiritual dimensions not only opens the door to
profound personal transformation but also challenges our fundamental understanding of reality itself. As we venture beyond the
confines of three-dimensional existence, we encounter philosophical concepts that question the very nature of our universe.

ONE SUCH CONCEPT IS NON-DUALITY, which suggests that ultimate
reality transcends dualistic distinctions such as good and bad,
self and other, or subject and object. Non-duality implies a
fundamental unity underlying all phenomena, where boundaries
dissolve, and separateness is revealed as an illusion. This perspective aligns closely with experiences reported by individuals

exploring higher dimensions, where the sense of individual identity merges with a greater cosmic consciousness.

QUANTUM ENTANGLEMENT, a phenomenon observed in quantum mechanics, offers another perspective on the interconnected nature of reality. According to quantum theory, particles that have interacted become entangled, such that the state of one particle instantaneously influences the state of its entangled partner, regardless of the distance between them. This interconnectedness suggests a fundamental unity underlying the fabric of reality, where everything is intricately linked in a vast cosmic web.

FURTHERMORE, the holographic nature of the universe proposes that reality is akin to a hologram, where each part contains the information of the whole. This holographic model implies that every individual consciousness is interconnected and contains the potential for infinite expansion and exploration. In the context of exploring spiritual dimensions, this suggests that each dimension reflects and contains the essence of all others, offering infinite pathways for self-discovery and evolution.

THESE PHILOSOPHICAL CONCEPTS challenge our conventional understanding of reality as static, linear, and separate. Instead, they invite us to embrace a more fluid, interconnected, and multidimensional perspective, where consciousness plays a central role in shaping our experience of reality.

THE EXPLORATION of spiritual dimensions confronts us with profound questions about the nature of reality and our place within it. Concepts such as non-duality, quantum entanglement, and the holographic nature of the universe invite us to reevaluate our understanding of existence and embrace a more expansive and interconnected worldview.

ETHICAL CONSIDERATIONS IN EXPLORING SPIRITUAL DIMENSIONS

While delving into the exploration of spiritual dimensions can be an enlightening and transformative journey, it's crucial to approach it with ethical considerations in mind. Here, we address some of the ethical considerations and potential pitfalls associated with navigating these realms, drawing upon insights from spiritual teachings and contemporary perspectives.

Discernment and Boundaries
Exercise discernment when engaging with spiritual practices and teachings. Not all sources of information are reliable or beneficial, so trust your intuition and critical thinking skills to evaluate the validity and integrity of the material.

GROUNDING PRACTICES: Maintain a strong connection to the physical realm and practice grounding techniques regularly. Grounding helps anchor you in the present moment and prevents you from becoming unbalanced or disconnected from reality.

MAINTAINING BALANCE WITH DAILY LIFE: Ensure that your exploration of spiritual dimensions is integrated with your daily life and responsibilities. Avoid becoming overly fixated on spiritual experiences to the detriment of your physical, emotional, and social well-being.

RESPECT FOR FREE WILL: Respect the free will and autonomy of others, especially when sharing spiritual insights or experiences. Avoid imposing your beliefs onto others or attempting to manipulate their spiritual journey. Instead, offer support and guidance when invited or requested.

SEEKING PROFESSIONAL GUIDANCE: If you encounter challenges or difficulties during your spiritual exploration, don't hesitate to seek support from qualified professionals, such as therapists, counsellors, or spiritual mentors. They can offer valuable guidance and assistance to help navigate any obstacles you may encounter.

CULTIVATING COMPASSION AND EMPATHY: Cultivate compassion and empathy towards yourself and others as you explore spiritual dimensions. Recognise that everyone's journey is unique, and be supportive and non-judgmental towards those with differing beliefs or experiences.

INCORPORATING these ethical considerations into one's spiritual practice fosters a sense of integrity, authenticity, and respect for the sacredness of the journey. By exercising discernment, practicing grounding techniques, maintaining balance, respecting free will, and embracing personal responsibility, individuals can navigate spiritual dimensions with greater clarity, compassion, and ethical conduct.

PRACTICAL EXERCISES FOR EXPLORING SPIRITUAL DIMENSIONS

Embarking on the journey of exploring spiritual dimensions can be a deeply enriching and transformative experience. To assist you in this exploration, here are some practical exercises and meditation techniques designed to help you connect with different dimensions firsthand:

DIMENSIONAL MEDITATION JOURNEY

- Find a quiet and comfortable space where you can relax without distractions.

- Close your eyes and take a few deep breaths to centre yourself.

- Begin by visualising a staircase in your mind's eye.

- With each breath, imagine yourself descending deeper and deeper into a state of relaxation.

- As you descend, set the intention to explore a specific dimension, such as the fourth or fifth dimension.

- Once you reach your desired dimension, allow your imagination to guide you as you explore this realm.

- Notice any sensations, images, or insights that arise during your meditation journey.

- When you feel ready, gently bring yourself back to the present moment and slowly open your eyes.

HIGHER SELF CONNECTION MEDITATION

- Sit or lie down in a comfortable position.

- Close your eyes.

- Take several deep breaths to relax your body and calm your mind.

- Visualise a radiant light above you, representing your higher self or spiritual essence.

- Feel this light descending from above.

- Allow the light to envelop you in its loving embrace.

- Merge with this light, feeling a sense of oneness and connection with your higher self.

- From this expanded state of consciousness, ask your higher self to guide you to a higher dimension or realm of existence.

- Trust in the wisdom and guidance that emerges during your meditation practice.

MULTIDIMENSIONAL VISUALISATION

- Set aside some time each day to practice multidimensional visualisation.

- Find a quiet space where you can sit comfortably and relax.

- Close your eyes and take a few deep breaths to centre yourself.

- Begin by visualising yourself surrounded by a sphere of protective light, shielding you from any negative energies.

- Then, imagine a doorway or portal in front of you, leading to a higher dimension or alternate reality.

- With each breath, feel yourself moving closer to this doorway, sensing the energy shift as you approach.

- When you feel ready, step through the doorway and into the unknown. Allow yourself to explore this new dimension with curiosity and openness, noticing any sensations, colours, or images that arise.

- When you're ready to return, simply visualise yourself stepping back through the doorway and into your present reality.

CHAKRA ACTIVATION FOR DIMENSIONAL TRAVEL

- Engage in chakra activation practices: Prepare your energy body for dimensional travel by activating your chakras.

- Focus on each chakra individually: Visualise them as spinning wheels of light along your spine.

- Start with the root chakra: Begin the activation process from the base of your spine.

- Work your way up to the crown chakra: Progress through each chakra, moving upwards towards the crown of your head.

- Infuse each chakra with vibrant energy and intention: Consciously channel energy into each chakra, imbuing them with purpose and vitality.

- Ensure all chakras are activated and aligned: Take the time to balance and align each chakra before proceeding.

- Set the intention to explore a specific dimension or realm: Clarify your intention for dimensional travel, focusing your mind on the destination.

- Feel yourself being lifted up by the energy of your activated chakras: Sensitise yourself to the energetic shifts occurring within your body as you prepare for dimensional exploration.

- Allow yourself to soar effortlessly into higher states of consciousness: Surrender to the process, trusting in the guidance of your activated chakras as you ascend into new realms of awareness.

These practical exercises are designed to assist you in your journey of exploring spiritual dimensions. Remember to approach these practices with an open heart and mind, allowing yourself to experience whatever unfolds with curiosity and acceptance. As you continue to explore and expand your consciousness, may you discover new realms of insight, wisdom, and spiritual growth.

RESOURCES FOR FURTHER EXPLORATION

To deepen your understanding and exploration of spiritual dimensions, here are some recommended resources:

Books:

- "The Power of Now" by Eckhart Tolle
- "The Astral Plane: Its Scenery, Inhabitants, and Phenomena" by C.W. Leadbeater
- "The Three Waves of Volunteers and the New Earth" by Dolores Cannon
- "The Fifth Dimension: An Exploration of the Spiritual Realm" by Vera Stanley Alder

ARTICLES:

- "Exploring the Multiverse: Scientific Concepts of Parallel Realities" (Scientific American)
- "Dimensions of Consciousness: Understanding Higher States of Awareness" (Psychology Today)
- "Navigating Higher Dimensions: A Practical Guide to Multidimensional Living" (Spirituality & Health Magazine)

ONLINE RESOURCES:

- Gaia.com: A platform offering a wide range of spiritual and metaphysical content, including documentaries, interviews, and instructional videos.
- The Monroe Institute: Provides programs and resources for exploring consciousness and altered states of awareness through techniques such as binaural beats and guided meditations.
- Institute of Noetic Sciences (IONS): Conducts research on consciousness, spirituality, and the interconnectedness of all life, with a focus on bridging science and spirituality.

BY ENGAGING WITH THESE RESOURCES, you can gain insights from both traditional spiritual teachings and contemporary scientific perspectives, allowing for a holistic and balanced exploration of spiritual dimensions.

INTEGRATION AND EMBODIMENT: LIVING A CONSCIOUS LIFE

REFLECTING ON THE JOURNEY

*W*elcome to the final chapter of our journey together—a voyage that has led us through the labyrinth of the chakras and into the realms of higher consciousness. But before we take the plunge into the waters of integration and embodiment, let us pause and reflect on the path we've embarked upon together.

FROM DELVING into the mysteries and evolution of the chakras to exploring the realms of higher consciousness, each step has been a sacred dance of discovery and awakening, intricately woven into the fabric and our cosmic journey.

IN EVERY MOMENT of exploration and revelation, we are not merely observers but active participants in the cosmic dance of creation, intimately intertwined with the rhythms of the cosmos.

Just as the energy that forms stars and planets resides within us all, we are connected to the divine tapestry of existence, embodying the very essence of the universe itself.

<small>TAKE A MOMENT TO PONDER:</small>

- What significant insights or breakthroughs have you experienced on your journey of exploring the chakras and spiritual dimensions?

- How have these insights influenced your perceptions of yourself, others, and the world around you?

- Have you noticed any shifts in your awareness, consciousness, or daily life practices as a result of your exploration?

- Which aspects of conscious living do you feel drawn to incorporate more fully into your life moving forward?

Now, as we prepare to integrate these insights into our daily lives, let us deepen our understanding of what it means to live a conscious and embodied existence.

BRINGING AWARENESS INTO DAILY LIFE

The first step in living a conscious life is to bring awareness to every moment. Mindfulness is the key that unlocks the door to deeper presence and connection. Close your eyes for a moment and visualise yourself at the beginning of this journey, full of curiosity and anticipation. Reflect on the experiences you've had, the lessons you've learned, and the growth you've experienced along the way. Now, imagine yourself embodying the principles of conscious living—radiating love, compassion, and authenticity in every interaction and decision.

MINDFUL PRACTICE

- Begin your day with a simple meditation or breathing exercise to ground yourself in the present moment. Throughout the day, practice bringing your attention back to the sensations of your body, the rhythm of your breath, and the beauty of the world around you. By cultivating this mindful awareness, you can infuse even the most mundane tasks with a sense of sacredness and purpose.

- Choose one daily activity that you often do on autopilot, such as washing dishes, commuting to work, or eating a meal. Commit to practicing mindfulness during this activity for the next week. Notice the sensations, thoughts, and emotions that arise without judgment, and observe how bringing awareness to this activity enhances your sense of presence and connection.

EMBODYING HIGHER CONSCIOUSNESS

Living a conscious life is not just about what we know intellectually; it's about how we embody and express that wisdom in our everyday actions. Take a deep breath and imagine yourself surrounded by a shimmering aura of light, representing the higher consciousness you are striving to embody. Feel the warmth and expansiveness of this energy as it fills every cell of your being. Now, think about a situation in your life where you can apply these principles—perhaps a challenging conversation or a decision that needs to be made. Visualise yourself responding with love, wisdom, and grace, knowing that you are aligned with the highest truth.

TAKE time to reflect on the values and principles that are most important to you—love, compassion, authenticity—and strive to align your thoughts, words, and actions with these higher ideals. Treat yourself and others with kindness and respect, and honour the interconnectedness of all beings. Remember, it's not enough to talk the talk; we must also walk the walk.

CULTIVATING PRESENCE AND CONNECTION

At the heart of conscious living lies the cultivation of deep presence and connection—with ourselves, with others, and with the world around us. Take a moment to connect with your breath, feeling the rise and fall of your chest with each inhale and exhale. Now, think about a loved one or a friend whom you deeply cherish. Visualise them standing before you, and imagine sending them waves of love, gratitude, and compassion from your heart to theirs. Feel the warmth and connection between you growing stronger with each breath.

PRACTICE TUNING into your inner guidance and intuition, trusting that it will always lead you in the right direction. Cultivate meaningful connections with friends, family, and community, nurturing relationships based on mutual respect, understanding, and support. Nurture practices such as heart-centred communication, active listening, and expressing gratitude.And don't forget to connect with the natural world,

163

spending time outdoors and immersing yourself in the beauty and wonder of the earth.

NAVIGATING CHALLENGES AND RESISTANCE

The path of conscious living is not always smooth sailing, and there will inevitably be challenges and obstacles along the way. When faced with difficulties, remember to approach them with an open heart and a curious mind. Take a deep breath and imagine yourself standing tall and grounded, like a mighty oak tree with roots reaching deep into the earth. Feel the strength and resilience of your spirit as you face whatever challenges come your way, knowing that you are supported and guided by the wisdom of your innermost being.

RATHER THAN RESISTING or avoiding discomfort, lean into it with courage and compassion, knowing that it holds the seeds of growth and transformation.

HERE ARE some practical tips to help you navigate common challenges encountered on the path of conscious living:

- **Managing Stress:** Stress is a common challenge in today's fast-paced world, but it doesn't have to derail your journey toward conscious living. Incorporate stress-relief techniques into your daily routine, such as deep breathing exercises, mindfulness meditation, or gentle yoga stretches. Taking regular breaks to rest and recharge can also help prevent burnout and maintain balance.

- **Dealing with Conflicts:** Conflicts are a natural part of human interaction, but they can disrupt our sense of peace and harmony. When conflicts arise, practice active listening and empathetic communication to foster understanding and resolution. Approach conflicts with an open mind and a willingness to find common ground, focusing on finding solutions rather than placing blame.

- **Maintaining Motivation:** Staying motivated on the path of conscious living can be challenging, especially when faced with setbacks or obstacles. Cultivate a sense of purpose by reconnecting with your core values and intentions regularly. Set small, achievable goals for yourself and celebrate your progress along the way. Surround yourself with supportive friends, mentors, or community members who inspire and encourage you on your journey.

REMEMBER, it's okay to stumble; what matters is how we pick ourselves up and keep moving forward. Practice self-care and self-compassion, and reach out for support when needed. By embracing challenges as opportunities for growth and learning, you can continue to evolve and expand on your path toward conscious living.

HONOURING PERSONAL GROWTH

Celebrate your growth and evolution on the spiritual path, no matter how small or incremental. Take a moment to acknowledge yourself for the courage and dedication you've shown in embarking on this journey of self-discovery and transformation.

Close your eyes and visualise yourself surrounded by a circle of light, representing the love and support of the universe. Feel the warmth and affirmation of this energy as it washes over you, filling you with a sense of pride and accomplishment.

EMBRACING THE JOURNEY AHEAD

As you continue to walk the path of conscious living, take time to honour and celebrate your growth and evolution. Celebrate the small victories and milestones along the way, recognising the courage and resilience it takes to step into your authentic self. Be gentle with yourself when you fall short of your ideals, knowing that you are always learning and growing. And above all, cultivate a sense of gratitude for the journey itself, knowing that every experience—whether joyful or challenging—is a precious gift that helps us to become more fully human. Embrace the present moment and the infinite possibilities that lie ahead.

WHILE THIS BOOK serves as a guide on your journey, it is merely a stepping stone towards deeper self-discovery and spiritual growth. I invite you to continue exploring and expanding your understanding beyond these pages. Seek out workshops, retreats, or online communities where you can connect with like-minded individuals and find ongoing support and guidance. Consider diving into additional resources such as books, articles, or podcasts that resonate with you and offer further insights into conscious living and spiritual awakening. Remember, the journey of self-discovery is lifelong, and there is always more to explore, learn, and experience.

AND SO, dear souls, in closing, I invite you to take a moment to place your hand over your heart and connect with the radiant light that dwells within you. Know that you are a beloved child of the universe, infinitely worthy and infinitely loved. As you go forth from this moment, may you walk in beauty, may you walk in grace, and may you walk in the light of your own divine essence. And may your journey be filled with love, joy, and boundless possibility.

The end.

Heart Chakra Phase 4 - The Power House

EPILOGUE

Reflecting on my journey, spanning three decades of meditation and exploration, I am deeply humbled. Through the transformative power of meditation and the healing resonance of sound, I've unearthed a profound synergy between the two.

In my quest to access states of lucid dreaming, I've found sound healing to be remarkably potent. The reverberations of the gong have served as keys, unlocking doorways to expanded consciousness and aligning me with higher frequencies.

It is my earnest hope that the insights I've shared resonate with you, igniting a spark within to illuminate your own spiritual journey.

I extend to you a heartfelt invitation to delve into your personal journey with greater introspection. Consider how the insights I've offered might intertwine with your own experiences, enriching your spiritual path.

Embrace curiosity, challenge conventions, and forge ahead, paving the way for progress. Remember, your journey of self-discovery is an everlasting voyage—may it be adorned with love, joy, and limitless exploration. Embrace empowerment and encouragement as your steadfast companions, guiding you through the twists and turns of your spiritual evolution. Each moment is a sacred opportunity for growth and transformation.

As you tread onward, may the light of inner wisdom illuminate your path, and may the transformative power of self-discovery be your guiding star. Walk with unwavering courage, boundless compassion, and authentic grace, knowing that each step you take brings you closer to your true essence. May your journey be adorned with abundant blessings, and may you discover profound peace, unbridled joy, and resounding fulfilment along the way.

REFERENCES

- Adyashanti. (2006). "The End of Your World: Uncensored Straight Talk on the Nature of Enlightenment." Sounds True.
- André, P., Ward-Thompson, D., & Barsony, M. (2000). From Prestellar Cores to Protostars: Observations of the Initial Conditions of Star Formation. Science, 288(5467), 25.
- Arnett, D. (1996). Supernovae and Nucleosynthesis: An Investigation of the History of Matter, from the Big Bang to the Present. Princeton University Press.
- Bahcall, J. N., Serenelli, A. M., & Basu, S. (2005). Solar Models: Current Epoch and Time Dependences, Neutrinos, and Helioseismological Properties. The Astrophysical Journal, 621(2), L85–L88.
- Barks, C. (2004). "The Essential Rumi." HarperOne.
- Blažinšek, K. (2017). "Ascension Symptoms: A Guide for Surviving the New World." CreateSpace Independent Publishing Platform.
- Bonan, G. B. (2008). Forests and Climate Change: Forcings, Feedbacks, and the Climate Benefits of Forests. Science, 320(5882), 1444–1449.
- Burbidge, G. R., Burbidge, E. M., Fowler, W. A., & Hoyle, F. (1957). Synthesis of the Elements in Stars. Reviews of Modern Physics, 29(4), 547–650.
- Cairns-Smith, A. G. (1985). "Seven Clues to the Origin of Life: A Scientific Detective Story." Cambridge University Press.
- Cannon, Dolores (2021) "The Three Waves of Volunteers and the New Earth" Ozark Mountain Publishing, Inc.
- Carroll, B. W., & Ostlie, D. A. (2007). An Introduction to Modern Astrophysics (2nd ed.). Pearson Addison-Wesley.
- Chopra, D. (1993). "Ageless Body, Timeless Mind: The Quantum Alternative to Growing Old." Harmony Books.
- Chopra, D. (1997). "The Seven Spiritual Laws of Success: A Practical Guide to the Fulfillment of Your Dreams." Amber-Allen Publishing.
- Chopra, D. (2013). "The Seven Spiritual Laws of Yoga: A Practical Guide to Healing Body, Mind, and Spirit." Hay House.
- Collings, P. J. (1990). "Introduction to Liquid Crystals: Chemistry and Physics." Taylor & Francis.
- Dale, C. (2013). "The Subtle Body: An Encyclopedia of Your Energetic Anatomy." Sounds True.
- Elias, M. (2015). Taoism: The Ultimate Guide to Mastering Taoism and Discovering True Inner Peace for Life! CreateSpace Independent Publishing Platform.

REFERENCES

- Evans II, N. J. (1999). The Formation of Stars. Annual Review of Astronomy and Astrophysics, 37(1), 311-362.
- Feuerstein, G. (1998). The Yoga Tradition: Its History, Literature, Philosophy and Practice. Hohm Press.
- Gienger, M. (2005). Crystal Power, Crystal Healing: The Complete Handbook. Sterling Publishing Company.
- Hall, J. (2011). The Crystal Bible: A Definitive Guide to Crystals. Godsfield Press.
- Hay, L. (1984). "You Can Heal Your Life." Hay House.
- Hunt, V. (1989). Infinite Mind: Science of the Human Vibrations of Consciousness. Malibu Publishing Company.
- Judith, A. (2004). "Eastern Body, Western Mind: Psychology and the Chakra System as a Path to the Self." Celestial Arts.
- Judith, A. (2004). Wheels of Life: A User's Guide to the Chakra System. Llewellyn Publications.
- Jung, C. G. (1964). Man and his symbols. Garden City, N.Y.: Doubleday.
- Kabat-Zinn, J. (2005). Guided Mindfulness Meditation Series 1. Retrieved from https://www.mindfulnesscds.com/collections/guided-mindfulness-meditation-series-1
- Kippenhahn, R., & Weigert, A. (1994). Stellar Structure and Evolution. Springer.
- Larson, R. B. (2003). The physics of star formation. Reports on Progress in Physics, 66(10), 1651.
- Leadbeater, C. W. (1927). "The Astral Plane: Its Scenery, Inhabitants, and Phenomena." Theosophical Publishing House.
- Leadbeater, C. W. (1927). "The Chakras." Theosophical Publishing House.
- Léon, A. (2006). "The Seven Initiations on the Spiritual Path." Llewellyn Publications.
- Léon, M. (2006). "The 5D Shift: The Five Dimensions of Consciousness." Simon & Schuster.
- Léon, O. (2006). "Crystals: Growth, Morphology, and Perfection." Cambridge University Press.
- Lynch, D. K., Livingston, W. C., & Van Hoven, G. (2002). Color and Light in Nature. Cambridge University Press.
- Orloff, J. (2010). "Emotional Freedom: Liberate Yourself from Negative Emotions and Transform Your Life." Harmony.
- Prialnik, D. (2000). An Introduction to the Theory of Stellar Structure and Evolution. Cambridge University Press.
- Raphael, A. (2016). "The Complete Book of Chakra Healing: Activate the Transformative Power of Your Energy Centers." Llewellyn Publications.
- Reference: Dharma Mittra quoted in Yoga Journal. (n.d.). "Unlocking Your Chakras: A Dharma Yoga Sequence." Retrieved from https://www.yogajournal.com/practice/yoga-sequence-for-the-chakras 24/03/2024
- Rossman, M. L. (2002). Guided imagery for self-healing. New York: H J Kramer.

- Simmons, R., & Ahsian, N. (2007). The Book of Stones: Who They Are & What They Teach. North Atlantic Books.
- Skoog, D. A., Holler, F. J., & Crouch, S. R. (2013). Principles of Instrumental Analysis. Cengage Learning.
- Stanley Alder, Vera (2000) "The Fifth Dimension: An Exploration of the Spiritual Realm" Weiser Books
- Stegall, J. (2018). "Energy Healing: Simple and Effective Practices to Become Your Own Healer." Althea Press.
- Sutton, G. P. (2000). Rocket Propulsion Elements: An Introduction to the Engineering of Rockets (7th ed.). Wiley.
- Tao, Z. (1984). The Tao of Health, Longevity, and Immortality: The Teachings of Immortals Chung and Lu. Element Books Ltd.
- Tolle, E. (2005). "A New Earth: Awakening to Your Life's Purpose." Penguin.
- Tolle, E. (2005). "The Power of Now: A Guide to Spiritual Enlightenment." New World Library.
- University of Colorado. (2022). Mineral Structures. Retrieved from https://chem.libretexts.org/Bookshelves/General_Chemistry/Map%3A_Chemistry_-_The_Central_Science_(Brown_et_al.)/13%3A_Properties_of_Solutions/13.1%3A_Types_of_Solids. (24/03/2024)
- Valentine, L. (1996). The Strength of the Mountain: Understanding Chinese Medicine. Paradigm Publications.
- Wauters, A. (2013). "Chakras and Their Archetypes: Uniting Energy Awareness and Spiritual Growth." Weiser Books.
- Wilber, K. (2000). "Integral Psychology: Consciousness, Spirit, Psychology, Therapy." Shambhala Publications.
- Wilcock, D. (2011). The Source Field Investigations: The Hidden Science and Lost Civilizations Behind the 2012 Prophecies. Dutton.
- Witten, E. (1995). String Theory Dynamics in Various Dimensions. Nuclear Physics B, 443(1-2), 85-126.
- Zhu, Y., Duan, X., Wang, J., Lu, X., Sun, X., & Cui, H. (2021). A comprehensive review on trace elements in human health and disease. Journal of Trace Elements in Medicine and Biology, 66, 126744. https://doi.org/10.1016/j.jtemb.2021.126744 (13/03/2024)

Contemporary spiritual teachings and practices that integrate chakra work with multidimensional exploration.

Articles:

"Exploring the Multiverse: Scientific Concepts of Parallel Realities" (Scientific American)

"Dimensions of Consciousness: Understanding Higher States of Awareness" (Psychology Today)

"Navigating Higher Dimensions: A Practical Guide to Multidimensional Living" (Spirituality & Health Magazine)

ACKNOWLEDGMENTS

A heartfelt thank you to my two wonderful sons, whose unwavering love and support have been the cornerstone of my journey. Your acceptance of my unique perspective on the world fills me with gratitude, and I cherish the love and friendship we share.

My sincere appreciation extends to all who have embraced this exploration into the realms of consciousness and the metaphysical. My deepest gratitude to you, the reader, for accompanying me on this voyage of exploration. Your dedication to this topic and interest in my words have been a constant source of encouragement and motivation. Thank you for being a part of this transformative journey.

I am also indebted to the multitude of philosophers, scholars, sages, and seekers whose documented journeys of discovery have illuminated our collective understanding of consciousness and its mysteries. While there are too many to name individually, their wisdom and inspiration have profoundly enriched our exploration.